Skene, Norman

The Design of Classic Yachts

Skene, Norman

The Design of Classic Yachts

ISBN/EAN: 9783867416771

First published in 2011 by Europaeischer Hochschulverlag GmbH & Co KG, Bremen, Germany.

© Europaeischer Hochschulverlag GmbH & Co KG, Fahrenheitstr. 1, D-28359 Bremen (www.ehv-online.com). All rights reserved.

This book is a reproduction of an out of print title and has originally been published in 1904. Because no electronic master copies of this title could be obtained, the publisher had to reuse old copies of the text. We therefore apologize for any possible loss in quality.

PREFACE

THIS book is intended to be a concise and practical presentation of the processes involved in designing a modern yacht. There is at present an almost utter lack of material of this character which is in accord with modern American practice, and it is thought that the book may find a useful place among works on yacht architecture. It is intended to be thoroughly practical in character, all mathematics and theoretical presentations having been eliminated as far as possible, so that the operations may be readily grasped by men without technical education.

A special feature of the book is the series of curves on plates VI, VII, VIII and IX, for determining the proportions of sailing yachts of various sizes. These have been prepared by the writer from data on a large number of yachts, and should prove of great assistance in roughing out a design. The methods presented for determining stability have been selected with reference to their applicability to small work, and are not ordinarily to be found in works on naval architecture.

The various operations involved in designing a sailing yacht are illustrated in the text by work on the thirty-foot water line sloop whose plans are given on plates I, II, III and IV. This is intended to be a conventional rather than an ideal design, and was chosen on account of its suitability for purposes of illustration. The complete data on this design is given in the appendix.

The author is indebted to Prof. C. H. Peabody, of the Massachusetts Institute of Technology, for criticism and suggestion.

N. L. S.

CONTENTS

CHAPTER I.

PAGE

GENERAL DISCUSSION................... I

CHAPTER II.

METHODS OF CALCULATION....... 5

CHAPTER III.

DISPLACEMENT 18

CHAPTER IV

THE LATERAL PLANE...................................... 24

CHAPTER V

DESIGN 28

CHAPTER VI.

STABILITY 33

CHAPTER VII.

BALLAST 48

CHAPTER VIII.

THE SAIL PLAN........... 54

CHAPTER IX.

CONSTRUCTION 59

APPENDIX.

TABLES 71

LIST OF PLATES

I. Lines of Thirty-Footer.

II. Construction Plan of Thirty-Footer.

III. Cabin   "   "   "   "

IV. Sail   "   "   "   "

V. Stability Figures.

VI. Curves of Ratios of Beam to Length.

VII.   "   " Draught.

VIII.   "   " Freeboard and Sail Area.

IX.   "   " Displacement.

ELEMENTS OF YACHT DESIGN

CHAPTER I.

GENERAL DISCUSSION.

THERE are four general characteristics sought after in yacht design—seaworthiness, large cabin accommodations, beauty and high speed.

These properties are in a measure antagonistic, and it is impossible to combine them all in one design, in fact seldom do we we see a successful combination of more than two of them. The best the designer can expect to do is to embody in his design the qualities especially desired, treating the other features in such a manner as to render their deficiencies as inconspicuous as possible.

In yacht designing one is less hampered than in any other branch of naval architecture, and the designer has many opportunities to depart from precedent and study the results of new ideas in design and construction. This is most fortunate, and to it may be attributed the great advance which has been made in the art in recent years.

The most marked development of form which has occurred is in the shape of the bow. This is the natural outcome of racing rules, which used water-line length as a basis of comparison. It was found that sail-carrying power could be increased independently of water-line length by increase of over-all length, especially in the bow. This increasing of the stability is the principal function of overhangs, and results from an increase in area of load water line plane and a general shifting to leeward of the center of buoyancy when heeled. There is scarcely any limit to the increase in stability which may be secured by lengthening and broadening the overhangs. This idea has been carried to such an extent as to render imperative the adoption of rules more stringent than those based simply on sail area and water-line length in order that boats of wholesome type may continue in the racing. Such rules are necessarily somewhat complex, and it is not until recently that any have been devised which were at all promising. The complete success of these rules has yet to be proved by extended use. As a temporary refuge against the machine racing boat a great deal of racing has been done in one-design and closely restricted classes. While these afford good racing they must be regarded in the light of a makeshift rather than a solution of the rating-rule problem.

They do not permit of much latitude of design, and for that reason are not of great benefit to the science of yacht architecture.

The problem of designing a sailing yacht with speed as a foremost consideration is a most complex one. External conditions to which a yacht is subjected, such as force and direction of wind, condition of sea, etc., are constantly changing so that the attainment of a given speed may not be sought but rather such a form as shall be easily driven at all speeds within appropriate limits. Nor is this the only consideration, for ease of form must be to some extent sacrificed for sail-carrying power. A harmonious adjustment between power and resistance should be sought. The problem of steam yacht design is much more simple, as there the hull may be so designed as to be most easily driven at the desired speed, for, contrary to early theories, the hull most easily driven at one speed is not most easily driven at all speeds. Then, again, the power-driven yacht travels ordinarily on an even keel and the form of the yacht need be but little affected by considerations of stability.

The resistance which a vessel encounters in passing through the water is made up of three kinds—frictional resistance, wave-making resistance, and eddy-making resistance.

Frictional resistance is the resistance due to the friction of the water on the surface of the vessel and depends upon the area of the surface, the nature of the surface, the length and shape of the surface. We are largely indebted to the late Mr. Froude for our knowledge of this form of resistance. Skin friction, as it is called, forms a large portion of the total resistance at low speeds, and is of course decreased by cutting down the area of wetted surface. It does not pay, however, to economize unduly on area of lateral plane for the sake of cutting down the area of wetted surface. It is obviously of great importance to have the immersed surface as smooth as possible.

Wave-making is a phenomenon, a full discussion of which would be out of place here. It is the chief source of resistance at high speeds and varies nearly as the displacement for similar forms. It is obvious that decreasing the displacement is the most effective way of cutting down resistance, other things being equal.

Eddy-making occurs at the stern post, if it is too wide, or at other places where the stream lines terminate abruptly, and is of slight importance in the ordinary yacht. The aft edge of centerboard, rudder, shaft struts, etc., should be well fined away to avoid the formation of eddies. The forward edge may simply be well rounded to avoid eddies at that point.

Let us now consider some types of racing boats produced under very lax restrictions. First, let us take the type developed where the length on the water line is the only restriction. The type found to be the fastest under these conditions is the extreme scow with enormous overhangs and carrying a very large amount of sail. The power to carry this rig is gained by great beam and over-all length. The weight of the crew contributes somewhat to the sail-carrying power, there being no ballast whatever. The overhangs are very broad and flat and project over the water at a very small angle with the surface. This permits the boat to gain length rapidly when heeled and greatly diminishes the retarding component of the impact of waves when going to windward. The waves strike the low overhang with great violence, but the blow is largely in an upward direction and does not tend to retard the boat as much as where the overhang presents a greater angle with the water plane. The wider and flatter the overhangs the less must be their angle of incidence with the water plane. To preserve the continuity of the very gradual lines of approach the entire underbody must be shoaled as much as possible. This compels a very small displacement and a reduction of weight wherever possible. The construction of this type of boat is the lightest possible and must be designed with great care to withstand the enormous stresses to which such a boat is subjected. An elaborate system of trussing furnishes the general strength, the hull proper being mere basket work.

Another type is that produced where the amount of sail to be carried is the only limitation. Here the problem is to produce the fastest possible hull for the given sail area and the stability is made merely sufficient to properly carry the sail under racing conditions. This is found to be a narrow, shoal, centerboard boat of extremely long and easy fore and aft lines, small displacement and consequent light construction. The stability is entirely that of form and of the weight of crew, there being no ballast whatever. The fastest type under the old rule

$$R. L. = \frac{L. W. L. + \sqrt{S. A.}}{2}$$

is probably a cross between the two just described. From the foregoing we may conclude that for considerations of speed alone the stability should be entirely that of form rather than of ballast.

The factors for speed which have been touched upon are unfortunately detrimental to safety and seaworthiness and for this reason are severely taxed by most rating rules. These commonly compel a certain displacement or weight of ballast and limit the amount of sail, the over-all length or the freeboard, and in other ways strive to produce a boat which shall be seaworthy as well as fast.

The form of the cruising boat has been influenced to an undesirable extent by the racing boat, and the prevailing type of small cruiser to-day is afflicted with long overhangs, shoal body, and pared away lateral plane. This is to be deplored, as such boats fall far short of the value they should possess as cruisers, considering the amount of money, labor and material put into them. There is no doubt that properly treated overhangs are of value in a seaway, but they must be short, high and fairly sharp in section. Water-line length has no bearing on the usefulness of a cruising boat. The modern boat of rational proportions has proved itself superior in every way to the plumb-stemmed and clipper-bowed craft of a few years ago, and the value of a moderate amount of overhang as a factor for seaworthiness is firmly established. The extensive adoption of generous overhangs on fishing schooners is evidence of this. Plenty of deadrise is desirable in a cruising boat, as it makes a boat easier in a seaway and affords more headroom in the cabin by permitting the floor to be placed lower down. The matter of lateral plane is discussed in a separate chapter.

CHAPTER II.

A LARGE proportion of the calculations of the naval architect revert to the determination of the area and position of center of gravity of a figure bounded by a curve. Two methods are in common use for these determinations, numerical and instrumenatal. The instruments used for the latter method are the planimeter and integrator. The planimeter measures areas alone. It is an inexpensive instrument, and is practically indispensable to the yacht designer. The integrator is a more expensive instrument, and while it is not indispensable for small work it is a practical necessity for large work where the saving of labor resulting from its use is very considerable. The integrator commonly measures areas and their moments about a given axis. Some integrators have in addition an attachment for measuring the moment of inertia of the area. Some of the uses of the planimeter and integrator will be explained later.

The principal methods of obtaining areas numerically are by the use of Simpson's first or one-third rule, and by the trapezoidal rule. Referring to fig. 1, let the area of the figure ABCD be required. AD is a straight

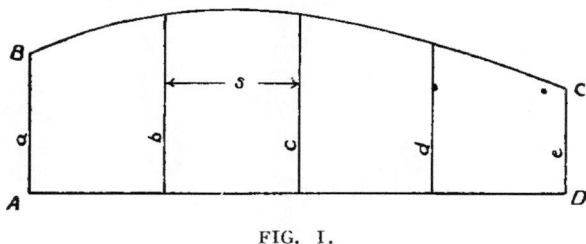

FIG. 1.

line, BC a smooth curve, and a, b, c, d, e, are ordinates drawn perpendicular to AD at a distance s apart. The area of the figure is then by Simpson's rule:

$$\text{Area} = \tfrac{1}{3}s \, (a+4b+2c+4d+e)$$

This rule may be used with any odd number of ordinates. To apply the trapezoidal rule, simply add together all the ordinates, subtract half the two end ordinates and multiply the sum by the common interval.   Referring to figure 1 the area by the trapezoidal rule is:

$$\text{Area} = s \; (\tfrac{1}{2}a + b + c + d + \tfrac{1}{2}e)$$

If the bounding curve started at A and ended at D, making the end ordinates zero, the area would be:

$$\text{Area} = s \; (b + c + d)$$

This rule may be used with any number of ordinates.

The trapezoidal rule deals with the figure as though it were bounded by a broken line—that is, in fig. 2 the area ABFG by the trapezoidal rule is equal to the sum of the trapezoids ABCJ, JCDI, IDEH, and HEFG.

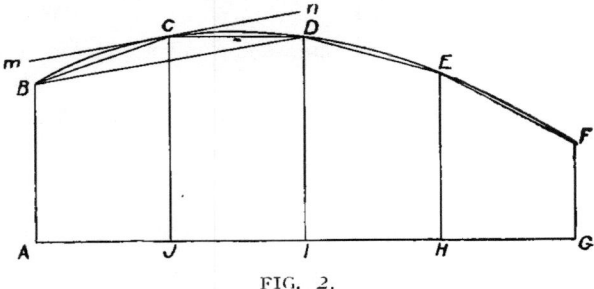

FIG. 2.

The area between BC, CD, DE, and EF and the curve is entirely neglected. This error is unimportant if the ordinates are sufficiently numerous, or if the curve is very flat. Where there is a reverse in the curvature the loss on the convex portion of the curve is offset partially or entirely by the gain on the concave portion. Simpson's rule assumes the portion of the curve BCD (fig. 2) to be an arc of a parabola tangent to mn (drawn parallel to BD) at C and the area BCD is added to, or subtracted from the area of the trapezoid ABDI, according as the curve is convex or concave.

For the purpose of comparing the two rules let us apply them to the segment of the circle shown in fig. 3.   This curve being entirely convex

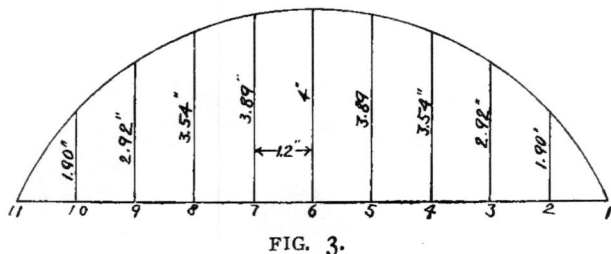

FIG. 3.

and steep at the ends shows the trapezoidal rule at its worst. The height of the arc is four inches and the length of the chord twelve inches, making the interval 1.2 inches with eleven stations. The calculation is as follows:

STATION	ORDINATE	SIMPSON'S MULTIPLIERS	FUNCTIONS OF AREAS
1	0	1	0
2	1.90	4	7.60
3	2.92	2	5.84
4	3.54	4	14.16
5	3.89	2	.7.78
6	4.00	4	16.00
7	3.89	2	7.78
8	3.54	4	14.16
9	2.92	2	5.84
10	1.90	4	7.60
11	0	1	0
Sum	28.50		86.76

Area by trapezoidal rule$=28.50\times1.2=34.20$ square inches.

Area by Simpson's rule$=86.76\times{}^{1.2}/_3=34.70$ square inches.

Knowing the radius of the arc the correct area of the segment is readily found by direct computation to be 34.63 sq. in. The errors then amount to 1.2 per cent. for the trapezoidal rule and 0.2 per cent. for Simpson's. The latter is in excess of the correct amount while the former is below.

In order to compare these rules still further the area and center of gravity of the curve shown in fig. 4 have been worked out by both rules.

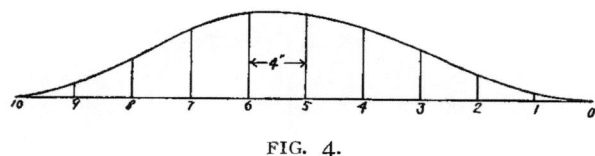

FIG. 4.

This is the curve of areas of a yacht having a prismatic coefficient of .51. The common interval is 4 inches. To obtain the correct area the trapezoidal rule with a very large number of ordinates was used giving 121.82 square inches. This area is of course still approximate but the error is almost infinitesimal and may be disregarded. The calculation is as follows:

<table>
<tr><td colspan="4" align="center">TRAPEZOIDAL</td><td colspan="6" align="center">SIMPSON'S</td></tr>
<tr><th>STA.</th><th>ORD.</th><th>ARM.</th><th>MOM.</th><th>STA.</th><th>ORD.</th><th>SIMP'S. MULTS.</th><th>FUNCS. AREAS</th><th>ARM.</th><th>FUNCS. MOM.</th></tr>
<tr><td>0</td><td>0</td><td>5</td><td>0</td><td>0</td><td>0</td><td>1</td><td>0</td><td>5</td><td>0</td></tr>
<tr><td>1</td><td>.48</td><td>4</td><td>1.92</td><td>1</td><td>.48</td><td>4</td><td>1.92</td><td>4</td><td>7.68</td></tr>
<tr><td>2</td><td>1.71</td><td>3</td><td>5.13</td><td>2</td><td>1.71</td><td>2</td><td>3.42</td><td>3</td><td>10.26</td></tr>
<tr><td>3</td><td>3.36</td><td>2</td><td>6.72</td><td>3</td><td>3.36</td><td>4</td><td>13.44</td><td>2</td><td>26.88</td></tr>
<tr><td>4</td><td>4.85</td><td>1</td><td>4.85</td><td>4</td><td>4.85</td><td>2</td><td>9.70</td><td>1</td><td>9.70</td></tr>
<tr><td>5</td><td>5.83</td><td>0</td><td>18.62</td><td>5</td><td>5.83</td><td>4</td><td>23.32</td><td>0</td><td>54.52</td></tr>
<tr><td>6</td><td>5.87</td><td>1</td><td>5.87</td><td>6</td><td>5.87</td><td>2</td><td>11.74</td><td>1</td><td>11.74</td></tr>
<tr><td>7</td><td>4.79</td><td>2</td><td>9.58</td><td>7</td><td>4.79</td><td>4</td><td>19.16</td><td>2</td><td>38.32</td></tr>
<tr><td>8</td><td>2.68</td><td>3</td><td>8.04</td><td>8</td><td>2.68</td><td>2</td><td>5.36</td><td>3</td><td>16.08</td></tr>
<tr><td>9</td><td>.83</td><td>4</td><td>3.32</td><td>9</td><td>.83</td><td>4</td><td>3.32</td><td>4</td><td>13.28</td></tr>
<tr><td>10</td><td>0</td><td>5</td><td>0</td><td>10</td><td>0</td><td>1</td><td>0</td><td>5</td><td>0</td></tr>
<tr><td></td><td>30.40</td><td></td><td>26.81</td><td></td><td></td><td></td><td>91.38</td><td></td><td>79.42</td></tr>
<tr><td></td><td></td><td></td><td>18.62</td><td></td><td></td><td></td><td></td><td></td><td>54.52</td></tr>
<tr><td></td><td></td><td></td><td>8.19</td><td></td><td></td><td></td><td></td><td></td><td>24.90</td></tr>
</table>

Area by trapezoidal rule $= 30.40 \times 4 = 121.60$ square inches.

Area by Simpson's rule $= 91.38 \times \frac{4}{3} = 121.84$ square inches.

Center of gravity by trapezoidal rule $= \frac{8.19}{30.40} \times 4 = 1.08$ inches to the left of sta. 5.

Center of gravity by Simpson's rule $= \frac{24.90}{91.38} \times 4 = 1.09$ inches to the left of sta. 5.

The percentage errors are then, for the trapezoidal rule, .24 per cent.; for Simpson's rule, .04 per cent. The difference in the positions of the center of gravity of the figure given by the two rules amounts to but .00025 of the base.

The process by which the center of gravity is found is briefly as follows: a station is selected near the middle of the length of base, in this case station 5, and each ordinate for the trapezoidal rule or function of areas for Simpson's rule is multiplied by the number of intervals between it and the station selected. These functions of moments are added separately on each side of the station about which moments are taken, the center of gravity being on the side of the larger sum. The difference of these sums divided by the sum of the ordinates for the trapezoidal rule or by the sum of functions of areas for Simpson's rule multiplied by the distance between stations gives the distance from the center of gravity to the station about which moments were taken.

The comparisons just made of the working of the trapezoidal and Simpson's rule show the latter to be the more accurate. The trapezoidal rule, however, is quite accurate enough if a sufficient number of stations are taken (nine or more are recommended) and will be used for all calculations in the ensuing pages. It is superior to Simpson's rule in that

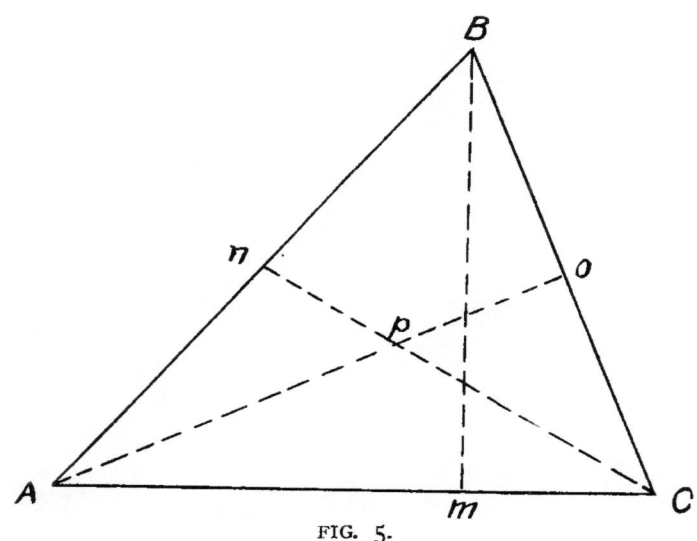

FIG. 5.

it may be used with any number of stations and involves much less numerical work in its application. These considerations more than atone for its being slightly less accurate. Some special calculations will now be presented.

The area of a triangle is equal to one-half the product of its base by its altitude, thus the area of the triangle ABC (fig. 5) is equal to ½ (AC × Bm). The center of gravity of the triangle is at p, the point of intersection of Ao and Cn, n and o being the middle points of AB and BC respectively.

The area of a quadrilateral having no two sides parallel is found by dividing the figure into two triangles and finding the area of each separately. Thus the area of ABCD (fig. 6) is equal to ½ (AC×Bm)+½(AC

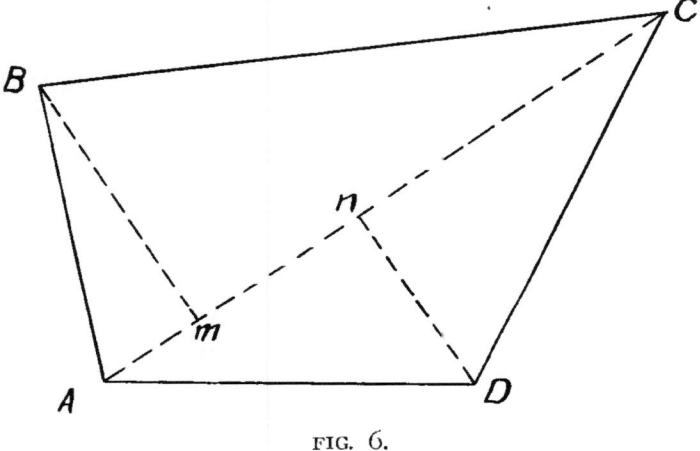

FIG. 6.

× Dn). The center of gravity is on a line connecting the centers of the component triangles. In fig. 7, m and n are the centers of the triangles ABD and BCD, while o and p are the centers of the triangles ABC and ACD. Draw lines mn and op. Their point of intersection, x, is then the

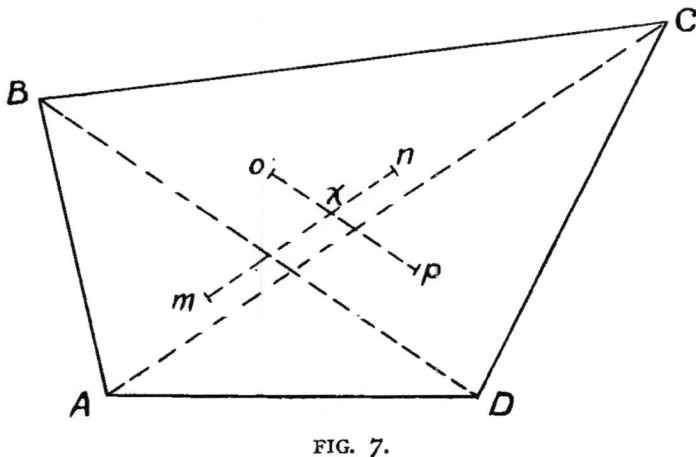

FIG. 7.

center of the figure ABCD. A somewhat quicker method of finding the
center of such a figure is shown in figure 8. Draw the diagonals Ac and
Bd. Lay off Cn=Am. Draw Bn. Bisect Bn and Bd, o and p being the

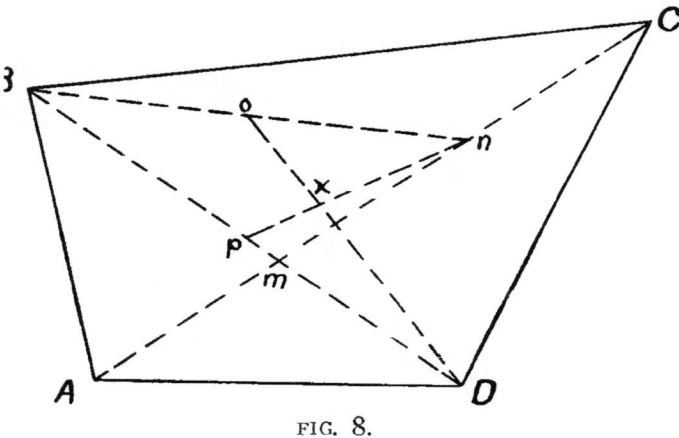

FIG. 8.

middle points. Draw Do and np. Their point of intersection, x, is the
center of gravity of the figure.

It is often necessary to find the common center of two areas or weights.
In fig. 9 let W and w represent two weights having their centers of grav-

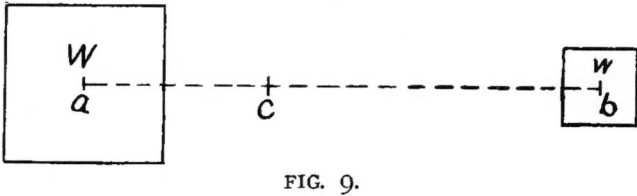

FIG. 9.

ity at a and b. Their common center lies at c on the line ab. Taking moments about a, the distance ac is equal to

$$\frac{w \times ab}{W+w}$$

There are various methods employed for finding the approximate area
of wetted surface of hull. These in general consist in applying Simpson's
or the trapezoidal rule to the half girths below the water line taken at
each station. The difficulty lies in determining the correct interval, as

the distance between stations on the surface of the skin is greater than at the centerline and is constantly varying. Taylor's mean secant method is probably the most accurate method for determining wetted surfaces. In applying Taylor's method each station is divided into a number of equal spaces below the water line as in fig. 10, where the lines MN and OP di-

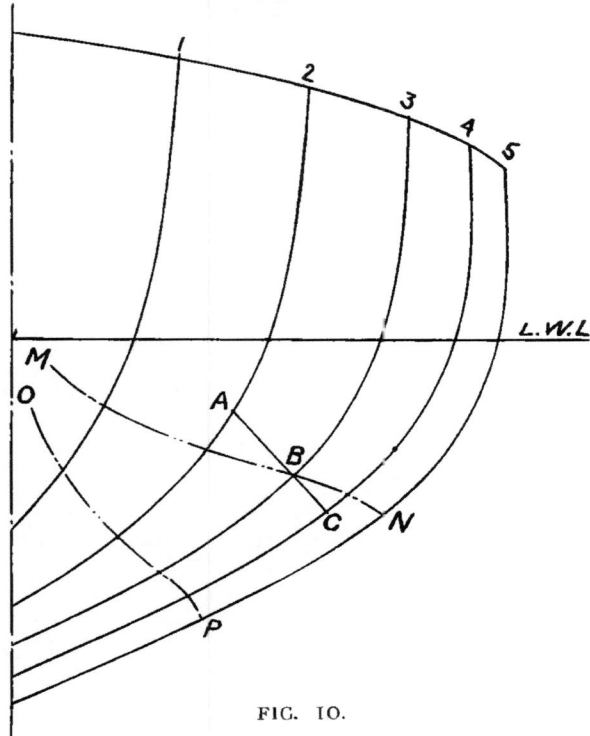

FIG. 10.

vide the stations into thirds. At a point B on station 3, the line AC is drawn normal to the station and stopping at A on 2 and C on 4. Now let us pass a plane through AC perpendicular to the plane of the paper. Fig. 11 shows this plane revolved into the plane of the paper. A'C is the projection of AC. If now we take a piece of paper and mark off on one edge of it the distance AA', which is twice the distance between stations, and then divide this distance decimally, we have a scale for measuring normals. If with this scale we measure AC fig. 10 (=A'C fig. 11) we have at once the tangent of the angle A' AC. Now in a table of natural functions find the secant corresponding to this tangent. The secant gives the distance AC in terms of AA'. Next find the distance AC in the same manner at the other points on the station and find their mean.

Multiply the half girth by this mean secant. Treat the half girth at each station in the same manner and sum up by the trapezoidal rule, using for s the actual distance between stations. The result is a very close approximation to one-half the wetted surface. Table I, of the appendix, gives tangents advancing by hundredths and the corresponding secants. The following

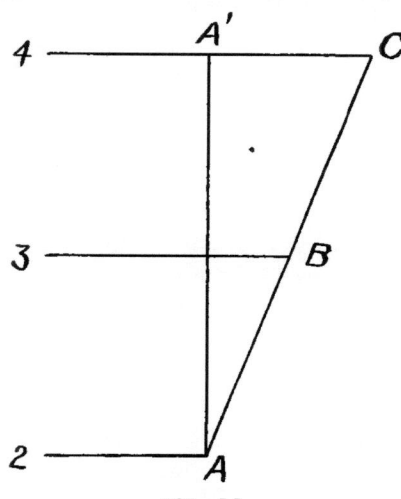

FIG. II.

calculation is for the wetted surface of the thirty-footer by Taylor's method.

SECANTS

STATION	4	5	6	7	8	9	10	11	12
At L. W. L.	1.038	1.036	1.026	1.016	1.003	1.000	1.006	1.018	1.026
" M N	1.033	1.028	1.016	1.007	1.001	1.000	1.007	1.024	1.031
" O P	1.031	1.024	1.016	1.008	1.001	1.001	1.011	1.006	1.028
" Keel	1.031	1.036	1.013	1.005	1.001	1.000	1.002	1.002	1.013
Sum	4.133	4.124	4.071	4.036	4.006	4.001	4.026	4.050	4.098
½ end ord.	1.035	1.036	1.020	1.011	1.002	1.000	1.004	1.010	1.020
Difference	3.098	3.088	3.051	3.025	3.004	3.001	3.022	3.040	3.078
Divide by 3	1.033	1.029	1.017	1.008	1.001	1.000	1.007	1.013	1.026
Half Girths	1.54	2.78	4.23	5.63	6.05	6.26	6.42	6.26	4.35
Corrected Half Girths	1.59	2.86	4.30	5.68	6.06	6.26	6.46	6.35	4.46

The corrected half girths are the products of the two preceding lines. The sum of the corrected half girths is 44.02. The wetted surface of the hull is then

$$44.02 \times \tfrac{4}{3} \times 2 \times 3 = 352.2 \text{ sq. ft.}$$

The factor $\tfrac{4}{3}$ corrects for scale, the half girths having been measured in inches on the drawing. The factor 2 allows for both sides and 3 is the distance between stations. To the immersed area of hull we must add that of rudder and centerboard. These are respectively 24.8 and 25.6, making the total area of wetted surface 402.6 sq. ft.

The application of Taylor's method is somewhat laborious and for small work the bilge diagonal method will do well enough. This method consists in taking the half girths as before and applying the trapezoidal rule using a corrected interval. This interval is obtained by multiplying the distance between stations by the length of a bilge diagonal between the stations at the forward and after points of immersion and then dividing by the length of the load water line.

To obtain the moment of inertia of a water line about its longitudinal axis measure the half-breadths at each station, cube them, apply the trapezoidal rule to the cubes of ordinates and multiply the result by two-thirds. If the ordinates are measured in inches, as is generally most convenient, and the drawing is to other than the one-inch scale, the sum of the cubes must be multiplied by the cube of the inverted scale. The cubes of ordinates should be taken from a table of cubes of numbers. The calculation for the moment of inertia of the L. W. L. of the thirty-footer about a longitudinal axis is as follows:

STA.	ORD. INCHES.	CUBES OF ORD.
4	1.43	2.92
5	2.52	16.00
6	3.31	36.26
7	3.91	59.78
8	4.29	78.95
9	4.37	83.45
10	4.19	73.56
11	3.74	52.31
12	2.88	23.89
		427.12

$$I = 427.12 \times \tfrac{2}{3} \times 3 \times (\tfrac{1}{3})^3 = 2025.$$

The factor 3 is the distance between stations and $(\tfrac{1}{3})^3$ corrects for scale, the ordinates having been measured in inches.

To find the moment of inertia of a water line about a transverse axis through its center of gravity we must first find the area of the water line and the position of its center of gravity. We may then find the moment of inertia of the water line about the midship section and make a correction to obtain the same about the center of gravity of the water line. Referring to the following computation on the thirty-footer we have in the second column the half-breadths of the load water line plane measured in actual inches on the drawing.

STA.	ORD.	ARM.	FUNC. FOR C. G. OF L. W. L.	ARM.	FUNC. FOR I
4	1.43	.5	7.15	5	35.75
5	2.52	4	10.08	4	40.32
6	3.31	3	9.93	3	29.79
7	3.91	2	7.82	2	15.64
8	4.29	1	4.29	1	4.29
9	4.37	0	39.27	0	0
10	4.19	1	4.19	1	4.19
11	3.74	2	7.48	2	14.96
12	2.88	3	8.64	3	25.92
	30.64		20.31		170.86

The third column gives the number of spaces each ordinate is from the midsection. The product of the second and third columns gives the functions for center of gravity of water line. The area of the water line is $30.64 \times 2 \times \frac{4}{3} \times 3 = 245.1$ sq. ft. The factor 2 allows for both sides, $\frac{4}{3}$ corrects for scale and 3 is the distance between stations. The center of gravity is

$$\frac{39.27 - 20.31}{30.64} \times 3 = 1.86 \text{ ft. for'd of sta. 9.}$$

Multiplying the functions for center of gravity again by the lever arms, we get the functions for moment of inertia. These are all added together and for the moment of inertia about station 9 we get $170.86 \times 2 \times \frac{4}{3} \times 3 \times 3^2 = 12302$.

The factor 2 allows for both sides, $\frac{4}{3}$ corrects for scale, 3 is the interval and 3^2 corrects for the lever arms, being in each case the number of intervals instead of the actual distance in feet between each ordinate and the midsection. Now to find the moment of inertia about the center of gravity of the water line we must subtract the area of the water line times the square of the distance between its center of gravity and the midsection. This correction is $245.1 \times 1.86^2 = 848$. The moment of inertia about the center of gravity is then $12302 - 848 = 11454$.

The calculation of the weight of the yacht is of great importance where there are definite limitations as to ballast and water-line length. The weight of each member should be calculated or estimated separately, the process for structural members being to find the volume and multiply by the density. Table II gives average values for the densities of various materials entering into the structure of the yacht. The volume of the planking is found by multiplying its area in square feet by its thickness in feet. The area is found in the same manner as the wetted surface, the half girths being taken from planksheer to rabbet line. The volume of the frames is found by multiplying the area of surface next the planking by the mean moulded depth. The area of outer surface depends on the siding and spacing, thus if the frames were sided two inches and spaced fourteen inches the area would be $^2/_{12} \times ^{12}/_{14} = ^1/_7$ that of the planking. The volume of the deck is found by multiplying its area, which is readily found, by its thickness. The volume of the beams is found in the same manner as that of the frames. The volume of the deadwood is found by applying the trapezoidal rule to the areas of transverse sections taken at regular intervals. The volumes of long members like stringers, clamps, spars, etc., are equal to the length multiplied by the mean sectional area. Table III gives the weights of spruce spars of various diameters. The most convenient methods of obtaining the weights of other portions of hull, rig and equipment will be apparent. Tables IV and V give weights of sails and fastenings. Care must be taken that nothing is omitted from the schedule of weights. There are some things such as paint, cabin fittings, personal effects, etc., which elude calculation and whose weight must be estimated. A fair allowance for outside paint is nine pounds per hundred square feet of surface over plain wood, nineteen pounds for canvas. The calculation of weights for the thirty-footer is given on page 50.

The accuracy of weight calculations on wooden boats is vitiated by the variation in densities of woods but with care, fairly close results may be obtained. This difficulty does not exist with the metal construction as the densities of plates and shapes are very accurately known and of course do not vary appreciably.

The plating of metal yachts is not of uniform thickness but is made heavier in localities which are especially stressed. For this reason the skin can not be dealt with as a whole but the weight of each plate or group of plates of the same weight must be figured separately. The dimensions of the plates should be taken from the shell expansion. The length however, is not shown correctly in the expansion and a correction should be made by multiplying by the secant of the angle which a diagonal through the given plates makes with the centerline. The weight of plates is expressed in pounds per square foot, and a forty-pound steel plate is considered to be an inch thick, making five pounds to the eighth of an inch. A bronze plate an inch thick weighs 43 pounds per square foot.

The length of frames and reverse frames should be measured on the body plan, making allowance for clips and doublings. The sum of the lengths of frames of the same size is to be multiplied by the weight per foot to get their weight. Weights of keels, keelsons, stringers and other longitudinal members may be found from their length, allowing for curvature, multiplied by their weight per foot. The weight of floors, deck stringer-plates, bracket and tie-plates may be calculated from their area and weight per square foot, allowing for lightening holes if any are cut. In finding the weight of deck beams their length should be measured along the upper crowned side and allowance should be made for the part turned down to form the bracket, if this construction is used. The weights of vertical laps, butt straps, liners under outer strakes and rivets may be computed, but the calculation would be very laborious, and it is customary to allow for these items by arbitrary percentages taken from practice. A fair allowance for these items is—butts, liners and rivets in plating, 10 per cent.; rivets in frames and reverse frames, 5 per cent.; rivets in floors and brackets 3 per cent.

Small yachts should be weighed after completion whenever possible as a check on the calculations. Naval vessels are often weighed during construction, that is, the weight of all the material worked into the ship is carefully recorded as well as the weight of all refuse taken out. This procedure might be employed to advantage in important yacht work.

Calculations for longitudinal strength and of stresses set up when among waves are sometimes made. As these calculations are very complex and are made only on very large or very lightly built steamers, it is thought unnecessary to give space to them here and the reader is referred to works on general naval architecture for these calculations.

In conclusion it may be said that the designer should avoid long hand figuring for computation, using logarithms or calculating machine exclusively, as otherwise, any extended calculation is so laborious as to render the work unprofitable. The ordinary slide rule is quite good enough for a large portion of the calculations on small yachts. Logarithms leave the work in a much more convenient form for reference than ordinary figuring and are especially valuable for finding powers and roots of numbers. In addition they are more expeditious and more accurate than ordinary figuring.

CHAPTER III.

DISPLACEMENT.

A NY object floating in water displaces its own weight, that is, if the object were placed in a vessel full of water, an amount would run over equal to the weight of the object. Displacement of yachts is commonly expressed in pounds up to 35 or 40 feet water line and in tons of 2,240 pounds above that size. The displacement is determined from the lines of the yacht as will be explained later. There are approximately 35 cubic feet of salt water and 36 of fresh water in one ton. In one cubic foot there are 64 pounds of salt water and 62.4 pounds of fresh water.

The center of buoyancy is the center of figure of the submerged portion of the vessel. The upward force of the buoyancy of the water may be considered to act at this point and the weight of the vessel to act at the center of gravity. The centers of buoyancy and gravity must be in the same vertical line or the vessel will alter its trim so as to bring them so.

In a yacht it is important to know the longitudinal position of the center of buoyancy when the yacht is erect, in order to be able to distribute the weights so that the yacht will trim properly. The vertical position of the center of buoyancy is not so important, athough a knowledge of its position is useful, as will be shown later. Its transverse position is, of course, in the central vertical plane.

If we plot the areas of the various transverse sections on a base line as in fig. 4. we have what is known as the curve of areas. The area of this curve gives us the displacement of the yacht, and the center of gravity projected on the base line gives us the longitudinal position of the center of buoyancy. The process of determining displacement and longitudinal position of the center of buoyancy is best explained by a concrete example, the calculation for the 30-footer being as follows: the quantities opposite the station numbers are the planimeter readings of each half section in square inches. The distance between stations is 3 feet.

	½ A SQ. IN.	ARM.	MOM.
4	.45	5	2.25
5	1.65	4	6.60
6	3.48	3	10.44
7	5.41	2	10.82
8	6.62	1	6.62
9	6.71	0	36.73
10	5.80	1	5.80
11	3.79	2	7.58
12	1.55	3	4.65
	35.46		18.03

Displacement $= 35.46 \times 2 \times {}^{16}\!/_{9} \times 3 \times 64 = 24207$ lbs.

$$C\ B = \frac{36.73 - 18\ 03}{35.46} \times 3 = 1.58' \text{ for'd sta. } 9 = 16.42' \text{ aft of sta. } 3.$$

The factor 2 is for both sides of the yacht, ${}^{16}\!/_{9}$ corrects for scale, 3 is the distance between stations required in the application of the trapezoidal rule, and 64 is the weight of one cubic foot of salt water.

The vertical position of the center of buoyancy may be found by taking the areas of water lines spaced at equal intervals from the load line down and summing up their moments in the same manner as for the longitudinal position. The vertical position is more readily found by the integrator if one be available, using the load line as an axis. The use of the integrator is described in chapter VI.

The determination of the proper displacement of a yacht is the most important step in laying out a design. The displacement must equal the sum of the weights of the various members of the yacht and its contents or the yacht will not float as designed. The logical procedure then is to ascertain the component weights and make the displacement equal to their sum. For a design where the limitations as to the water-line length and amount of ballast are very stringent, the best procedure is to lay out a preliminary design which shall have the proper displacement and general dimensions as nearly as it is possible to estimate them and to then make calculations for weight on this design as outlined in chapter II. The displacement for the final design will then be made equal to the sum of these weights. For cruising boats it does well enough to estimate the proper displacement from data on successful boats of similar type and after calculating the weight, to assign an amount of ballast to supply the deficiency of weight. If the proper displacement is known fairly close and a portion or all of the ballast is to be carried inside, the calculation for weight may be dispensed with as the amount of weight is easily adjusted to secure the desired flotation. The curve of displacement on plate IX will serve as a guide in estimating displacement for sailing yachts.

The best position for the center of buoyancy is something of which very little is known. An examination of the data for a large number of representative existing yachts shows its position to lie generally between 50 to 56 per cent. of the load water-line length from its forward end. From 52 to 54 per cent. is a suitable position for cruising boats.

The fineness of a design is commonly represented by three coefficients. These are the midsection coefficient or ratio of midsection to the circumscribed rectangle, the block coefficient or ratio of the volume of the displacement to the volume of the circumscribed parallelopipedon and the prismatic coefficient or ratio of the volume of the displacement to the volume of a solid whose length is equal to the length of the water line and having a constant sectional area equal to that of the mid section. It is also the ratio of the area of the curve of the transverse areas to the area of the circumscribed rectangle. The last coefficient is the most important for our purposes. The area of midship section cf the thirty-footer is

$$6.80 \times 2 \times {}^{16}\!/_{9} = 24.2 \text{ sq. ft.,}$$

and the prismatic coefficient is equal to

$$\frac{24207}{30 \times 24.2 \times 64} = .522.$$

For steam yachts and launches, the prismatic coefficient generally lies between .54 and .60. For centerboard boats having little external keel it varies from .53 to .61. • For boats of the semi-keel type from .50 to .54 For the modern keel boat it varies from .46 to .50. Having decided on a suitable prismatic coefficient for a design the area of the midsection is readily calculated for a given displacement as follows

$$A = \frac{D \text{ cu. ft.}}{LWL \times PC}$$

The form of the curve of areas is a matter of considerable significance, as it shows the manner in which the displacement is distributed longitudinally. A design may be perfectly fair and sweet yet have an undesirable distribution of the displacement as revealed by the area curve. The form of the curve has undoubtedly great influence on the wave-making resistance and should of course be that of least resistance for a given displacement and speed. According to the wave-form theory as proposed by Colin Archer in 1877, the curve should take the form of a wave line. A discussion of resistance and the wave-form theory would not accord with the purpose of this book, and the application of the theory to yacht design will simply be given. The wave form theory requires the curve of areas to be a curve of versed sines for the forebody or .6 of L. W. L. and a trochoid for the afterbody. The length of forebody in well-formed yachts is generally between 54 and 58 per cent. of the water-line length, that is, the midsection or point of greatest sectional area is in the neighborhood of 56 per cent. of the water-line length from the forward end.

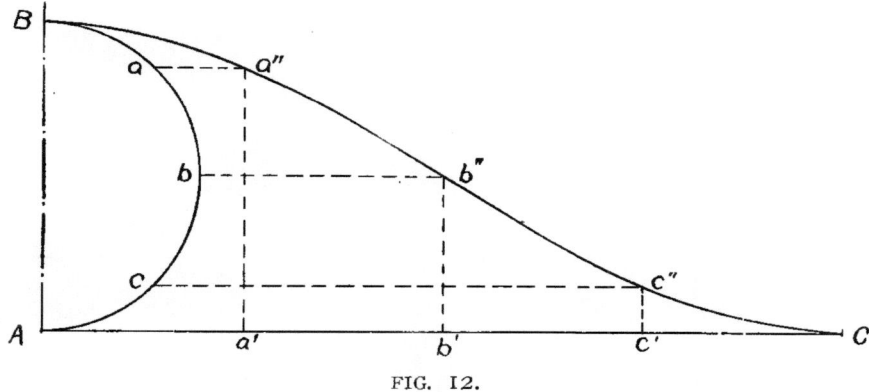

FIG. 12.

Before proceeding further it will be well to give the construction for the curve of versed sines and the trochoid. Suppose in fig. 12 it is desired to construct a curve of versed sines of length AC. Let AB be the diameter of generating circle. Divide the semi-circumference into a number of equal divisions. Divide the base line, AC into the same number of equal divisions. Draw lines parallel to AC through a, b, c, and perpendiculars through a', b', c'. The points of intersection a'', b'', c'', lie on the curve. Fig. 13 shows the construction for the trochoid. The semi-circumference and base line are spaced off as before. Draw the chords Aa, Ab and Ac. Draw a'a'', b'b'', c'c'', parallel and equal to the chords Aa, Ab and Ac. The points a'' b'' c'' lie on the curve. The area of the versed sine curve is always equal to one-half product of base line by diameter of generating circle, that is, its coefficient is .5. The trochoid has a varying coefficient dependent on the ratio of diameter of generating circle to base line, the coefficient increasing with the ratio. The height of the trochoid may be increased to pass through any desired point, having first drawn it with the proper diameter of generating circle to give the desired coefficient, by multiplying each ordinate by the height at the point through which the curve is to pass divided by the ordinate of the original curve at the same point.

There is undoubtedly an advantage in having the area curve conform to the wave-form theory. Its importance, however, should not be over-estimated, as this in itself will not produce a speedy design, and, on the contrary, many successful yachts have a curve differing widely from that

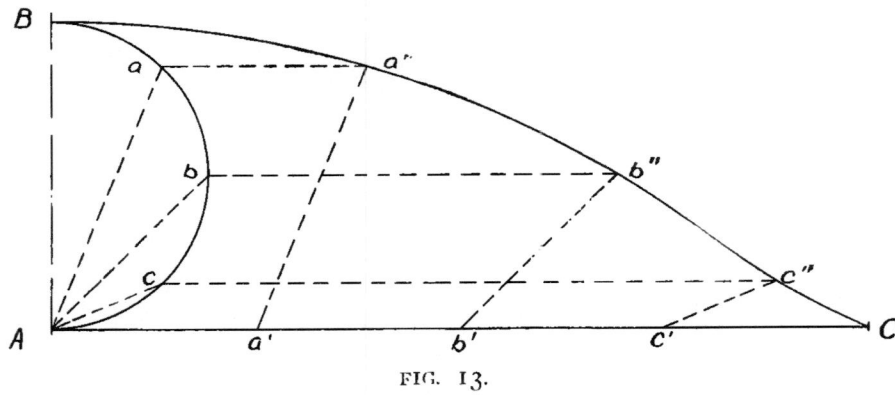

FIG. 13.

prescribed by the wave-form theory. The area curves of steam yachts and centerboard boats having little external keel may be made to take an exact wave form, decreasing, however, the length of forebody from .60, the water line length to .56 or .57 to accord with modern practice. In boats having a pronounced external keel it is desirable to treat boat and keel separately, making the areas of the boat proper take the wave form. Table VI gives a series of factors for constructing wave-form curves having various prismatic coefficients.

To construct an area curve using these factors divide the base line between the forward and after points of immersion into ten equal parts. Erect ordinates at these points, and having selected a suitable prismatic coefficient, multiply the area of midship section by the factors of the curve having that coefficient and plot these quantities on the ordinates. A curve through these points will have the wave form and its prismatic coefficient and position of center of buoyancy will be as indicated in table VI. Curves having other prismatic coefficients may readily be constructed by using various other ratios of diameter of generating circle to base. An excellent method of design is to start with the curve of areas and make the areas of transverse sections conform to the curve. In this way all irregularities in the curve are avoided and the displacement and position of center of buoyancy are sure to work out as intended after the design has been faired up. This method of designing from the area curve is explained more fully in chapter V.

CHAPTER IV.

THE term lateral plane is applied to the vertical, longitudinal projection of the under-water body of the vessel. The center of lateral resistance is the point at which the lateral pressure of the water on a boat sailing close-hauled may be considered to be concentrated. It is practically impossible of determination and is considerably farther forward than the center of figure of the lateral plane. The reasons for this are that as the boat moves forward it is constantly entering solid water, increasing the pressure at the bow and decreasing it toward the stern where the water is more or less disturbed. The wave which is piled up under the lee bow tends also to increase the pressure in the region of the bow. Moreover, the contour of the lateral plane when the yacht is heeled is quite different from that in the erect position. The position of the center of buoyancy is also considered to affect the position of the center of lateral resistance.

Since we cannot determine the true center of lateral resistance we must assume a center for reference in placing the center of our sail plan. The center of lateral plane is generally used for this purpose, although some designers use a center lying on a line between the centers of buoyancy and of the fin or centerboard, disregarding entirely the hull in shoal-bodied boats. This point probably bears a more constant relation to the true center of lateral resistance than the center of lateral plane. In either case the proper distance fore and aft from the reference point to the center of the sail plan must be determined experimentally from existing boats of the given type.

It is found that to secure satisfactory results the fore and aft position of the center of lateral plane must lie within certain definite limits. Its position is commonly located with reference to the forward point of immersion, its distance from that point being expressed in terms of the water line length. In most yachts this distance is between 54 and 58 per cent. of the water line. In the majority of cases 56 or 57 per cent. will give the best results. In cases where the center of the sail plan is necessarily very far aft, as in the old-fashioned catboats, the center of lateral plane may be placed as far back as 60 or 61 per cent. Very small centerboard craft often have their centers very far forward with apparently good results. In centerboard boats it is well to have the center of the board somewhat ahead of the general center so that when the board is raised the general center may move aft, making the boat steer better off the wind.

The necessary amount of lateral plane is something for which no very definite rules can be stated, as it varies greatly with the type of boat; thus a centerboard boat requires relatively less lateral plane than a keel boat, as the centerboard being a plane surface is more effective in resisting lateral pressure than the somewhat rounded surface of the keel. The type of rig and amount of sail carried also have a bearing on this question. A convenient comparative method of approximating the area of lateral plane is by the ratio of lateral plane to area of midsection. This ratio worked out for a large number of representative yachts is found to vary from 4.0 to 6.0. The higher ratios are found in the clipper-bow type with a long keel, entirely convex in contour. For keel boats of ordinary type the ratio should lie between 4.25 and 5.50. Centerboard boats may in general have a slightly smaller ratio than keel boats of similar type. For illustration, the thirty-footer has an area of midsection of 24.2 sq. ft. Taking a ratio of 4.65 the area of the lateral plane should be approximately 24.2 × 4.65 = 112.5 sq. ft.

Bilge boards are much more effective in resisting lateral pressure than a centerboard as they are nearly vertical when the boat is heeled down beating to windward and present a surface normal to the direction of pressure. On this account the area of each bilge board may be made much less than the necessary area of a centerboard for the same boat (about .7 as great). The decreased wetted surface and capsizing tendency of bilge boards commend their use on shoal racing boats.

Designers differ as to whether the rudder should be considered a part of the lateral plane or not, but the best practice is to disregard it and the figures given above for area and center of lateral plane are for the plane exclusive of rudder. In a properly balanced yacht there is but little pressure on the rudder when sailing by the wind, and for this reason the rudder can hardly be considered a factor in resisting lateral pressure. An exception may be made in some types such as catboats, where it is impracticable to secure a proper balance by placing the rig far enough forward. The angle of weather helm and consequent loss of speed in such boats is reduced by increasing the area of the rudder so that the rudder may be considered lateral plane when comparing boats of this type. The area of rudder required varies widely with different types. Its size may be advantageously stated in terms of the area of lateral plane exclusive of rudder or ratio of rudder to lateral plane. Table VII gives suitable values of this ratio for various sizes and types of yachts. Selecting a ratio of .11 for the thirty-footer we get for area of rudder $112.5 \times .11 = 12.4$ sq. ft.

The shape of the lateral plane has great influence on the performance of the yacht. The modern tendency is toward a concentration of the plane fore and aft. This has its advantages for racing boats as such a plane is more efficient and consequently may have less area and less wetted surface than one whose area is more widely distributed fore and aft. Quick turning is another advantage pertaining to this type. The fact that those features of design tending to produce speed are detrimental to seaworthiness when carried to a high degree holds true in the case of the lateral plane and for this reason the fore and aft concentration of lateral plane should be avoided on cruising boats. Boats with this type of plane have a tendency to fall off and steer badly in a heavy sea, they must be finely balanced and carefully steered at all times, their balance is greatly affected by reefing and varies with different strengths of wind. If a boat is to lie hove to well the lateral plane must be well spread out in a fore and aft direction.

The forward portion of the lateral plane is most effective for lateral resistance, and for this reason the leading edge should be made as long as possible. To carry out this idea the keel bottom should have considerable drag or slope, as then the leading edge extends from the bow aft to the rudder and is constantly entering solid water all along its length.

The exact form of the calculation for area and center of lateral plane depends on the character of the design. If the plane is regular in contour, the trapezoidal or Simpson's rule may be used. If such a plane has a centerboard the areas and centers of hull and board should be found separately and the combined center found by taking moments about a convenient point. In the case of a very irregular contour the plane should be divided into a number of portions in such a way that the area and center of each may be readily figured. Moments of each are then taken about a convenient point, the sum of the moments divided by the sum of the areas giving the distance from the point to the total center. The cardboard method of determining the center of lateral plane is susceptible of sufficient accuracy if used with care, and is much more expeditious than calculation. The calculation of area and center of lateral plane of the thirty-footer is as follows: the first column gives measurements on each station in inches from the water line to the keel bottom.

STA.	ORD.	ARM.	MOM.
4	.60	5	3.00
5	1.27	4	5.08
6	2.40	3	7.20
7	3.35	2	6.70
8	3.50	1	35.0
9	3.60	0	25.48
10	3.73	1	3.73
11	3.85	2	7.70
12	2.36	3	7.08
	24.66		18.51

$$\text{Area} = 24.66 \times \tfrac{1}{3} \times 3 = 98.64 \text{ sq. ft.}$$

Distance center is forward of station $9 = \dfrac{6.97}{24.66} \times 3 = .85$ ft. or 17.15 ft. aft of 3.

This area neglects a small triangle at the forefoot between stations 6 and 7, also one at the after end of keel between stations 11 and 12. It is too great by the amount of the triangle whose hypothenuse is a straight line from the water line on 14 to the stern post on 12. These errors are due to the fact that the trapezoidal rule assumes the figure to be straight between ordinates. To make these corrections let us take moments about station 3.

$$98.64 \times 17.15 = 1692$$

1st triangle	$.86 \times 10.50 =$	9
2nd "	$1.67 \times 25.35 =$	42
	101.17	1743
3rd "	$1.32 \times 28.64 =$	38
	$99.85 \times 17.07 = 1705$	

The center of lateral plane exclusive of centerboard is 17.07 ft. abaft sta. 3 or 56.9 per cent. The board has an area of 12.80 sq. ft. and its center is 16.70 ft. back. Taking moments of hull and board

$$99.85 \times 17.07 = 1705$$
$$12.80 \times 16.70 = 214$$
$$\overline{112.6 \times 17.04 = 1919}$$

The total C. L. P. is then 17.04 ft. abaft sta. 3 or 56.8 per cent.

CHAPTER V.

DESIGN.

BEFORE starting a design it is well to fix upon the principal dimensions which include length over all, at the water line, beam at water line, extreme draught, area of lateral plane, displacement and area of midship section. Having settled upon the type and water-line length, the other proportions are generally arrived at by some sort of comparison with existing boats. As an aid in making such comparisons the curves on plates VI, VII, VIII and IX have been prepared. These curves are based on data taken from a large number of successful existing yachts and may be considered thoroughly representative of current American practice. Plate VI gives ratios of beam at water line to length on water line for cruising boats, and plate VII gives extreme draughts. For this work yachts have been divided into three classes, viz., keel boats with all outside ballast, semi-keel boats with a small centerboard and all or nearly all the ballast outside, and centerboard boats having all or nearly all the ballast inside. It will be noted that the differences between the types so marked in the smaller sizes disappear almost altogether in the larger boats. The small sizes vary greatly as to beam and draught and the first part of the curves simply represents a fair average value for these quantities. In general, a boat having greater beam than is shown by plate VI, will have less draught than is indicated on plate VII for the same water line length and vice versa. The larger sizes of yachts conform more closely to the curves. Plate VIII gives curves of sail area and least freeboard to top of rail. It was found impracticable to make any distinction for type in drawing these curves. Plate IX gives average values for displacement, being expressed in pounds up to forty feet water line and in tons of 2,240 pounds above that size.

These curves will be found of great value in blocking out the proportions of a new design. By their use comparison is made of the proportions of a large number of existing yachts of the given size instead of with only one or two as is generally the case. It is understood that these curves apply only to cruising boats. It should not be inferred that the dimensions of a well-proportioned boat must lie on or very near the curves, as many excellent designs show quite a divergence from them, especially in the smaller sizes. On the other hand, if the proportions indicated by the curves for the given water line length are adhered to, a design may be produced which will be of excellent proportions in the light of present practice.

In order to illustrate the process of laying out a design, the procedure followed in the case of the thirty-footer will be given. Having settled upon a thirty-foot water line, semi-keel cruiser of normal proportions, the principal dimensions were taken from the curves as follows: the ratio of beam at water line to water-line length as indicated on plate VI is .385. The beam then should be $30 \times .385 = 11.55$ ft. or about 11 feet 7 inches. Plate VII gives slightly over five feet draught at 30 feet water line. Plate VIII gives for the least freeboard 2.43 feet or about 2 ft. 5 in. The displacement curve shows about 24,000 pounds at 30 feet water line. 24,200 pounds was taken as a safe figure. The next step is to determine the proper area of midsection to give this displacement. A suitable prismatic coefficient for this type of boat is .50 to .52. Using .52 the area of midsection should be

$$\frac{\dfrac{24200}{64}}{30 \times .52} = 24.2 \text{ sq. ft.}$$

The half area in square inches on the drawing will be $24.2 \times \frac{1}{2} \times \frac{9}{16} = 6.81$ sq. in. The area of lateral plane should be about $24.2 \times 4.65 = 112.5$ sq. ft. as explained on page 25.

We now have sufficient data to enable us to block out the design. It will be assumed that the reader has some knowledge of lines and is familiar with meaning of the terms elevation, half-breadth plan, body plan, etc. The first step is to draw the profile using the least freeboard, draught, area and center of lateral plane already fixed upon. It is a good plan to draw a preliminary profile at half the scale of the lines and enlarge the final profile from that. The object in doing this is to reduce the drawing to such a size that the eye can take in the entire drawing at a glance and study the way in which each portion harmonizes with the whole. A very good way is to draw the sail plan first. In this way the effect of the rig on the general appearance of the boat may be studied and the sheer line, profile of bow and stern, etc., drawn so as to harmonize in the best manner. On the preliminary profile the freeboard at bow and stern and the length and contour of the overhangs are determined. The contour of lateral plane may also be drawn in on this plan, being altered and redrawn until area and center come as intended. The final profile may then be enlarged from the preliminary sketch.

The midship section should be drawn in next at the proper distance from the forwarl point of immersion. This distance was made 56 per cent. of the water-line length=16.81 ft. for the thirty-footer. The section is drawn with the water-line beam, draught and area already assigned and with the height of rail and draught given by the profile at that point. The shape of the section is of great importance, as it influences the form of the entire boat. The most suitable shape of midship section is found by experience. It must possess the elements of speed, stability and seaworthiness combined in the proportions best adapted to the type of boat in hand. In general, the shoal flat section contains the elements of speed in higher degree than a narrower and more V-shaped section. This is within certain limitations and has numerous exceptions.

Having drawn in the midsection, we may next direct our attention to the half-breadth plan. The midsection gives us a point amidships through which to draw the sheer or deck line. The best shape for this line is also

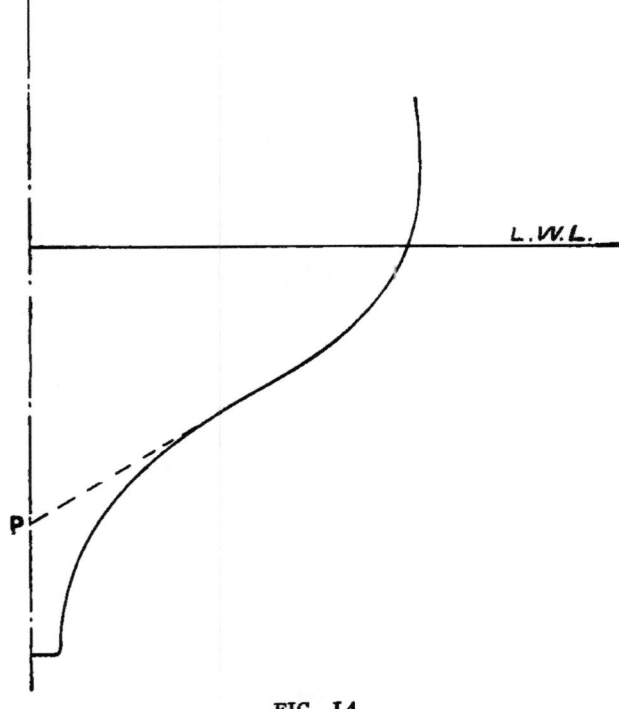

FIG. 14.

a matter of judgment based on experience. It is a good plan generally to have the widest point on deck a little abaft the widest point at the load line giving what is known as the raking midship section. A preliminary load water line may be drawn next and the half-breadths at deck and load line transferred to the body plan. We now have three points on each station on the body plan through which to draw the transverse sections, the top of planksheer, load water line and keel bottom. The usual procedure from this point is to draw in the stations by eye, fair them up, draw a displacement curve and see if the displacement comes out near enough. A much better method is to draw an arbitrary displacement curve to start with and make the area of each station conform to that indicated by the curve for that station. This course was pursued in designing the thirty-footer. It is somewhat difficult to preserve the area of the section during the process of fairing up, but it may be done with care and practice. Where the yacht has an appendage, as is usually the case, we must deal with the areas of sections above the centerline. By centerline is meant a line passing through the points P on each section (fig. 14), where the prolongation of the flat of the bottom intersects the central plane. The areas above centerline are the areas above the dotted line, all below that line being considered the appendage.

The thirty-footer's half area of midsection in square inches on the drawing is 5.89. A boat of her type should have a prismatic coefficient for the portion above centerline of about .52. In constructing the curve of areas above centerline, the factors in column 2, table VI were used. This gives for areas of half sections above centerline in square inches:

STA.	½ MID SEC. SQ. IN.	FACTORS	½ A SQ. IN.
4	5.89	.080	.47
5	"	.285	1.68
6	"	.560	3.30
7	"	.808	4.77
S	"	.972	5.73
9	"	.983	5.79
10	"	.823	4.85
11	"	.507	2.98
12	"	.167	.98

The stations were drawn and altered until the area of each was as indicated above and these areas were adhered to in fairing up. The curve of areas above centerline is drawn in on plate I with the curve of areas below centerline superposed. This shows very markedly the decided bump amidships in the curve caused by the appendage.

Having drawn in and faired the upper body the appendage may be drawn in and its displacement computed. A slight variation in the displacement of the appendage is easily effected in order to bring the total displacement to the desired figure.

A brief outline of the process of fairing lines may be of value at this point. The design is faired by taking sections through the boat in varous planes, longitudinally on water lines, buttocks and diagonals and transversely on the stations. After the transverse sections have been drawn in as nearly fair as possible by eye, the diagonals, buttocks, etc., are developed and the sections are altered until all these developments are perfectly fair curves. The operation of fairing should be commenced with those longitudinal sections whose planes are most nearly perpendicular to the contour of the transverse sections. These are generally the diagonals. Having faired the boat by the diagonals, the water lines or buttocks are developed next. It is important to take a sufficient number of these, as a boat may be apparently perfectly fair by the diagonals and yet exhibit peculiar places in the ends when the water lines come to be drawn in and vice versa. The intersections of water lines and buttocks in the elevation must correspond with those in the plan. The procedure is varied somewhat according to the type of boat; thus in a shoal, flat craft some of the buttocks would be developed first. The designer, as he gains experience, varies the procedure and adopts methods which he has found of especial value to him.

The practice of making a model from the lines is to be recommended, as sometimes slight imperfections in the design are made apparent by the model, where it would be difficult or impossible to detect them in the lines. The practice of making the model first and the lines from the model is now practically obsolete.

After the completion of the design the computations for weight, stability, etc., should be made in order to ascertain whether or not the design will fulfill requirements in a satisfactory manner. These computations are dealt with elsewhere. The final operation is to take offsets from the design from which to lay the boat down full size in the mould loft.

CHAPTER VI.

STABILITY.

THE statical stability of a vessel is the moment of the couple formed by the weight and buoyancy. In fig. 15 W L is the water line in the erect position, W' L', the water line, when heeled to the angle θ under the action of the wind or some other force, B, the position of the center of

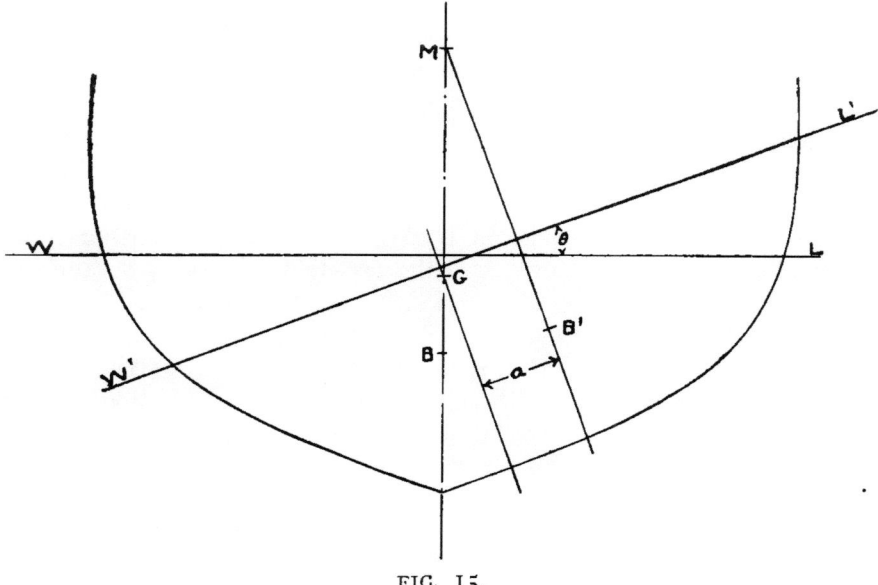

FIG. 15.

buoyancy in the erect position, B' the position of the center of buoyancy when heeled to the water line W' L'; G is the position of the center of gravity and a is the distance between lines passing through G and B' perpendicular to W' L'. The intersection at M of the perpendicular through B' with the centerline is known as the metacenter; G M is called the metacentric height. As long as G is below M the stability is positive, that is, the vessel will tend to return to the erect position when inclined. With G at M the stability is said to be neutral and with G above M the stability is negative and the vessel will take an inclination until it reaches a position where G is below M.

The transverse statical stability of a yacht is equal to the displacement multiplied by a, the righting arm. The process of determining the stability at any angle of heel consists then in finding the distance apart of the centers of gravity and of buoyancy in a direction parallel to the water line at that angle. It is evident that the stability is dependent upon two factors. that of weight and construction as affecting the position of G and that of the form of hull as affecting the position of B'.

The center of gravity, G, lies of course on the centerline of the yacht in the erect position. Its vertical position cn that line may be found by direct calculation, by approximation and by experiment on the completed yacht. The calculation for vertical position of the center of gravity is similar to that for longitudinal position as performed in chapter VII. The weights of the component members of the structure and equipment are found together with their vertical distances from a reference line, usually the base line or load water line. The moments of the weights are summed up and divided by the total weight, giving the distance of the center of gravity from the reference line. This is a very laborious process, too much so for ordinary small yacht work, and it is simpler and generally sufficient to arrive at the position of the center of gravity by an approximation. A simple method of approximating its position is to divide the weight of the yacht into several portions, as, for instance, the weight of the rig taken at the center of effort, the hull proper taken at the center of its profile, the deadwood taken at its center of profile, and the lead keel taken at its center, which may be computed or estimated closely. Adding the moments of these weights about the water line and dividing by the total weight, we have a very close approximation to the correct position of the center of gravity. The application of this approximation to the thirty-footer is as follows:

ABOVE L. W. L.

ITEM	WT.	ARM.	MOM.
Rig	1200	21	25200
Hull	8980	.8	7180
Equipment	1800	0	0
Crew	600	3	1800
	12580		34180

BELOW L. W. L.

ITEM	WT.	ARM.	MOM.
Deadwood	1820	3.0	5460
Lead	9800	4.1	40200
	11620		45660

$$\text{C. G. below L. W. L.} = \frac{45660 - 34180}{12580 + 11620} = .474 \text{ ft.}$$

After the yacht is built and afloat the center of gravity may be accurately located by an inclining experiment. Inclining experiments should be performed whenever possible, as the knowledge of the position of the center of gravity obtained in this way is of great assistance in approximating the position for a new design of the same type. Let us consider, first, the case where an inclination is produced by raising a quantity of ballast or other weight from the hold to the deck and then moving it outboard.

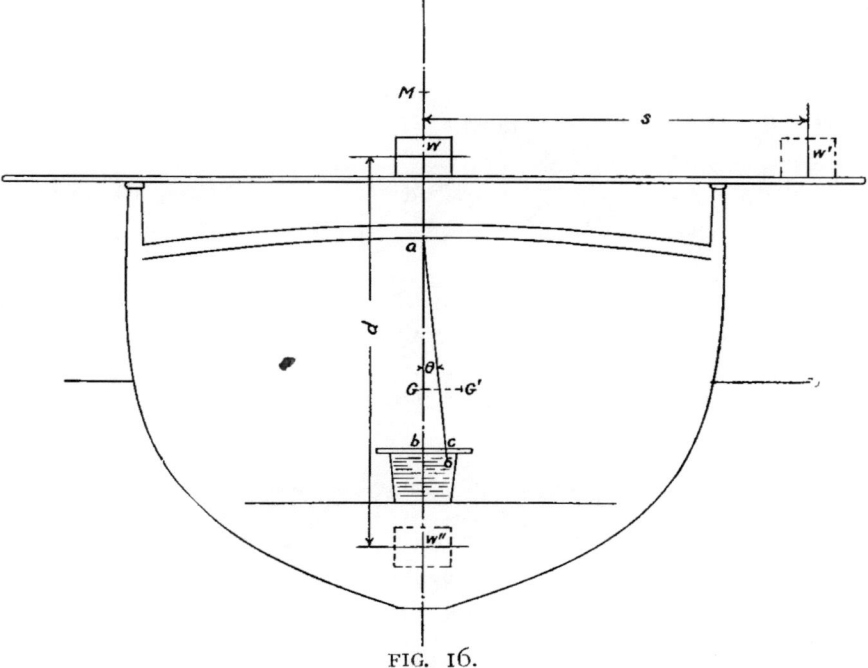

FIG. 16.

In fig. 16 w is the weight which has been raised from the hold where it occupied the position w″. With the weight at w, the center of gravity is at some point G. Now if the weight is moved outboard a distance s, to the position w′ the center of gravity moves from G to G′, causing an angle of inclination θ, which is indicated by a plumb bob attached to a deck beam at a. It is a good plan to have the plumb bob hang in a bucket of water as shown so as to steady it. The distance it swings b c is noted on a stick across the top of the bucket.

Now the distance GG', which the center of gravity has moved is equal to

$$\frac{w \times s}{\text{Disp.}}$$

M is the position of the metacenter and is found by computation from the lines as explained later, then

$$GM = GG'Cot\theta = \frac{w \times s}{\text{Disp.}} \times \frac{a\ b}{b\ c}$$

a b and b c are readily measured, so that we may solve for G M giving us at once the height of the center of gravity with the weight on deck at w. If d is the distance w has been raised, the center of gravity with w at w'' will be lowered by the amount

$$\frac{w \times d}{\text{Disp.}}$$

Where there is no weight aboard which may be used for inclining the yacht it is necessary to employ some weight which is not a portion of the yacht's equipment. Let M be the position of the metacenter calculated for the immersion with his extra weight aboard. Then as before

$$G\ M = G\ G'\ Cot\theta = \frac{w \times s}{D+w} \times \frac{a\ b}{b\ c}$$

which gives G as the position of the center of gravity with weight on board. Now with the removal of the weight, the center of gravity will be lowered by the amount

$$\frac{w \times h}{\text{Disp.}}$$

where h is the height of w above G.

The experiment should be conducted on a still day in a location where there is no sea or current. All bilge water should be pumped out and no one besides the observer should be aboard when the readings are taken. After taking a reading the weight should be shifted to the other side an equal distance from the center line and a second reading taken. Two different inclinations should be used, taking a double reading for each. The angles should be from one to three degrees.

For small angles (up to about 10 degrees) the height of M remains practically constant. The righting arm is equal to G M $\sin\theta$ and the stability equals D$\times$G M $\sin\theta$.

We have then simply to determine the metacentric height in order to find the stability ; this is known as the metacentric method of determining stability and is applicable only to very small angles of inclination.

The height of the metacenter above the center of buoyancy is equal to the moment of inertia of the water-line plane divided by the volume of the volume of the displacement or

$$B\ M = \frac{I}{V}.$$

As the demonstration of this is somewhat complicated it is deemed inadvisable to give space to it here, and the reader is referred to works on theoretical naval architecture for this demonstration. We have seen in Chapter II, page 14, how to determine the moment of inertia of a water line about its longitudinal axis. For the thirty-footer, the transverse moment of inertia of the load water line works out at 2025. The height of the transverse metacenter above the center of buoyancy is

$$B\ M = \frac{I}{V} = \frac{2025}{378.2} = 5.36 \text{ ft.}$$

378.2 is the displacement in cubic feet. Now GM=BM—BG so that we have to locate B and G in order to determine G M. The methods of determining the heights of the centers of buoyancy and of gravity have already been dealt with. In the 30-footer, the center of buoyancy is very nearly one foot below the center of gravity and the righting arm at 10 degrees is then, by the metacentric method, about 4.36$\times$.174=.76 ft.

The metacentric height for longitudinal inclinations is analagous to that for transverse inclinations and is found in the same way with the difference that the moment of inertia of the water line is taken about a transverse axis through its center of gravity. As worked out on page 15, the longitudinal I for the thirty-footer, is equal to 11454 and B M is then equal to

$$\frac{11454}{378.2} = 30.29 \text{ ft.}$$

It is evident that for small inclinations the metacentric height is a measure of the stability. This leads to a consideration of suitable values of G M for various classes of yachts. In racing yachts, where the sail area is unlimited, the metacentric height is made as great as possible either by placing the center of gravity very low or by greatly increasing the moment of inertia of the water line. A large metacentric height represents great stiffness and tendency to return quickly to the upright from small inclinations. This causes violence of motion when among waves and is to be avoided in power-driven craft where the steadying effect of sail is absent. It is a popular error that great stiffness is essential to a comfortable power craft. On the contrary, boats having very small metacentric heights are often the most steady at sea. This holds in a way in the case of sailing yachts, and for this reason cruising yachts have in general smaller metacentric heights than racing boats. The value of G M for steam yachts of about 100 feet water line should be about 1.5 feet, for steamers of 200 feet water line it lies in the neighborhood of 2 feet.

As stated, the amount of metacentric height is an indication of the stability for very small angles only, and for this reason cannot be used for determining sail-carrying power and is no indication of the range of stability. It is especially useful in investigating the condition of steamers in various states, such as without coal in the bunkers, with coal and stores aboard, and in the launching condition. In order to have a complete knowledge of the stability of a yacht, we must determine the lengths of righting arm at various and wide angles of heel. If we plot these values as ordinates, using angles of heel as abscissæ, we have a curve of righting arms. This curve for the thirty-footer is shown in fig. 1, plate V. From this curve the length of righting arm for any given angle of heel is readily interpolated. The actual stability or righting moment is, of course, obtained by multiplying this righting arm by the displacement. The points to be noted in a stability curve are the angle at which the stability is a maximum, the amount of stability at that angle and the range of stability. The curve of the thirty-footer shows a range of 127 degrees, or greater than could possibly occur from effects of wind pressure alone. Many heavily-ballasted keel racing boats have a range of stability of 180 degrees, the stability at no time being negative. On the other hand lightly-ballasted centerboard boats, while having large metacentric height and great stability at small angles, have a limited range, reaching their limit sometimes at as low as 50 or 60 degrees.

The amount of stability at small angles, as obtained from the metacentric height, is dependent solely upon the position of the center of gravity and the form of the underbody. At large angles, however, the amount of freeboard and general form of the upperbody plays a very important part. An increase of beam increases the height of the first part of the curve of righting arms, while an increase of freeboard increases the length of the curve.

There are numerous methods of determining stability at large angles of heel, most of which are too cumbersome and laborious in their application to be of value for yacht work. The three methods, a discussion of which follows, have been selected with especial reference to their applicability to small yacht work. These methods are:

1. Blom's Method. This a purely mechanical method, and consists in pricking off on very thin card from a tracing of the body plan, the shape of the underwater portions of evenly-spaced transverse sections at a given angle of inclination and up to a water line cutting off the required displacement. These are pasted lightly together in their correct relative positions and their common center of gravity determined. This is done by suspending the sections from two or more points at the edge of the card and noting where plumb lines from the points of suspension intersect. This point is the center of buoyancy at that angle and the distance between the centers of buoyancy and of gravity in a direction parallel to the water line is easily measured. If this process is pursued for other angles at intervals of about 10 degrees, we may then draw a curve of righting arms.

2. Heeled Longitudinal Sections.

This method is by direct computation, and as an example of its application, the righting arm for the thirty-footer at 20 degrees heel, has been worked out. The work is recorded in the table on page 40.

In fig. 2, plate V, the water lines, W' L' and W''' L'' are drawn so as to cut off the same displacement as W L and represent an angle of heel of 20 degrees. Longitudinal sections perpendicular to W' L' and W'' L'' are drawn at a, b, c, etc. The sections are spaced a foot apart, and section g passes through the center of gravity G, found by the approximation, already given. Referring to the table, the measurements recorded in the columns headed a, b, c, etc., are the distances in feet from the inclined water line to the intersection of the longitudinal and transverse sections. By drawing two inclined water lines W' L' and W'' L'', we avoid the necessity of drawing a double body plan like fig. 3. Measurements for the forebody are taken from W' L' as far as section h and from W'' L'' for sections i and j. Measurements for the afterbody are taken from W'' L'' as far as section i with the exception of station 12 on section h, where the distances from the first to the second intersection by h is measured. Sections i and j are measured from W' L'. After the measurements are all taken, the

MEASUREMENTS ON SECTIONS

Sta.	a	b	c	d	e	f	g	h	i	j
4				.06	.39	.50	.49	.70		
5		.66	.52	1.00	1.13	1.10	1.22	2.86	.65	
6		1.58	1.41	1.73	1.83	1.82	1.94	4.08	1.26	.37
7	.11	2.13	2.07	2.22	2.26	2.27	2.53	4.26	1.72	.66
8	.88	2.22	2.41	2.47	2.48	2.54	2.87	4.41	1.72	.67
9	1.20	1.92	2.47	2.50	2.50	2.55	2.87	4.16	1.18	.33
10	.85	1.35	2.20	2.27	2.22	2.22	2.52	3.69	.33	
11	.10	.63	1.68	1.72	1.66	1.58	1.96	.24		
12			1.03	1.06	.90	.74	1.22			
13			.32	.35	.18					
Sum	3.14	10.49	14.11	15.38	15.60	15.32	17.62	24.40	6.86	2.03
Area	9.42	31.47	42.33	46.14	46.80	45.96	52.86	73.20	20.58	6.09

SUMMARY

Sec.	Area	Arm	Mom.
a	9.42	6	56.82
b	31.47	5	157.35
c	42.33	4	169.32
d	46.14	3	138.42
e	46.80	2	93.60
f	45.96	1	45.90
g	52.86	0	
h	73.20	1	73.20
i	20.58	2	41.16
j	6.09	3	18.27
Sum	374.85		

661.17

132.63

Righting Arm at 20° Heel $= \dfrac{661.17 - 132.63}{374.85} = 1.41'$

columns are added and their sums multiplied by the spacing of the stations, in this case three feet, give the areas of the sections a b c, etc., in square feet by the trapezoidal rule. The areas are then transferred to the column at the right headed areas, and added together. The sum of the areas multiplied by the spacing of the sections (1 foot), gives for the heeled displacement 374.85×1×64=24000 lbs.

The area of each section is multiplied by its distance in feet from g, the section passing through the center of gravity G, and the moments on each side of g are then added separately. The difference of the sums of moments divided by the sum of the areas of sections gives 1.41 feet for the length of the righting arm at 20 degrees.

3. The Mechanical Integrator. The use of the integrator reduces greatly the amount of labor in making stability calculations, and for this reason is now used practically to the exclusion of numerical methods, by naval architects, who have much stability work to do. Fig. 17 is a diagram of a common form of the instrument. The integrator runs on a steel track T. P is the tracing point. The disc at A records area readings, and disc M records moment readings. Some forms of the instrument have still another disc for finding moment of inertia of plane figures.

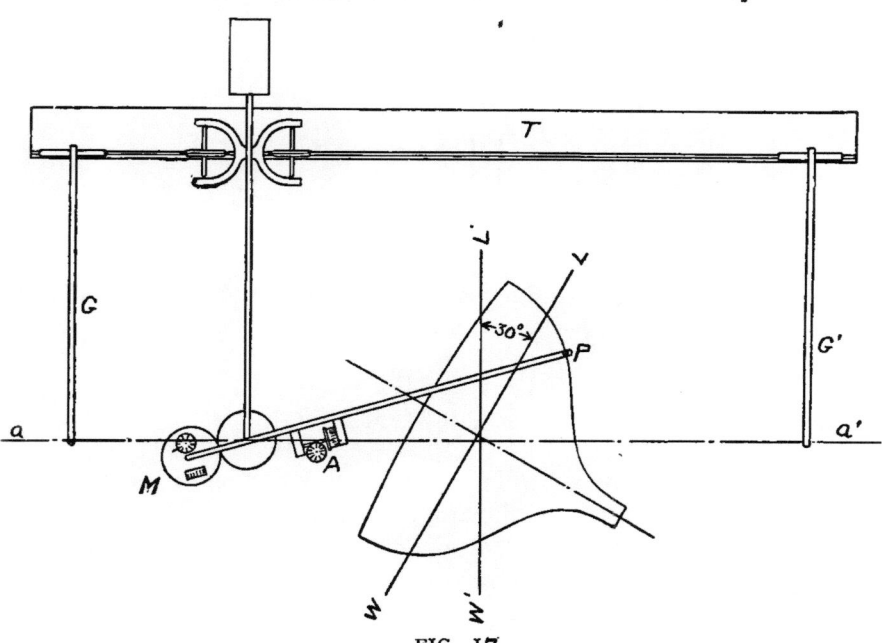

FIG. 17.

In using the integrator, the track is first set parallel to and at the correct distance from the axis of the figure by means of the gauges G and G'. In figure 17 the instrument is placed for finding the righting arm of a yacht at 30 degrees inclination. The line a a' is the axis about which moments are taken. This line passes through the center of gravity G, and makes an angle of 30 degrees with the centerline. Although it is convenient to have the axis pass through the center of gravity, it is not essential, for a correction in length of righting arm is readily made as shown

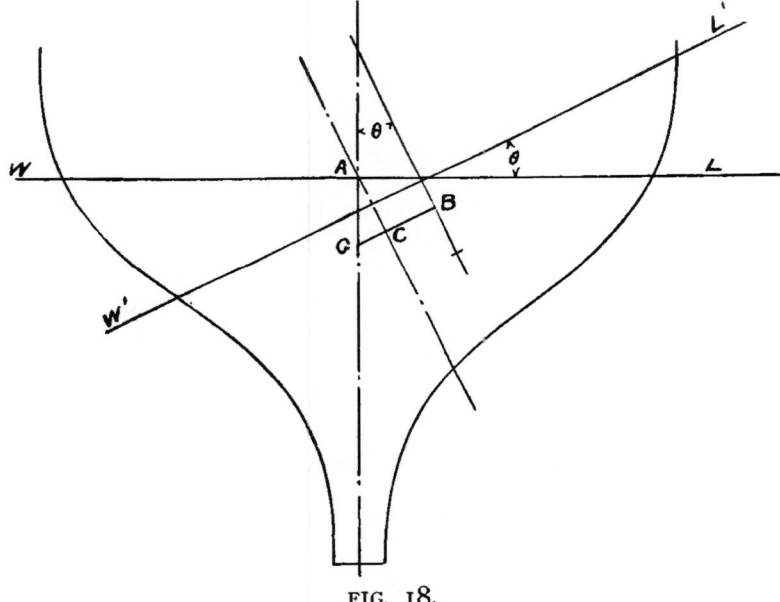

FIG. 18.

in fig. 18. Suppose the righting arm about an axis A C is found to be C B. Now if the center of gravity is at G, the true righting arm will be

$$G B = C B + G C$$
$$= C B + G A \sin\theta$$

that is, if the center of gravity is below the intersection of the axis with the centerline, we must add to the arm as found the distance from G to intersection with the axis times the sine of the angle. If G is above the intersection, G A $\sin\theta$ is to be subtracted.

If we set the discs of the integrator at o, and then sweep the tracing point around a transverse section, we may take readings of the discs which, when multiplied by the constants of the instrument, give us the area and moment of the section. The moment divided by the area gives the distance from the axis to the center of the section. If this is done for all the sections of the boat and the areas and moments of the sections summed up, we may get the displacement and righting arm. The application of this method requires a double body plan such as is shown in fig. 3, plate V. In that figure the afterbody is drawn in dotted to avoid confusion.

The area and moment readings may be taken and recorded separately, but an easier and quicker way is to sweep the tracing point around each of the sections in succession, without stopping to take readings until all have been traced. Care must be taken not to omit any sections. The final readings give the sum of the areas and moments of the sections. These readings have simply to be corrected for the constant of the instrument and for scale before finding displacement and arm.

The sums of the moment and area readings for the thirty-footer at 20 degrees inclination were respectively 19.00 and 34.99. The constants of the instrument were 4 for moments and 2 for areas. The righting arm is equal to

$$\frac{19.00 \times 4 \times {}^{64}/_{27}}{34.99 \times 2 \times {}^{16}/_{9}} = 1.45 \text{ ft.}$$

${}^{64}/_{27}$ corrects the moment reading for scale, being the cube of the inverted scale ${}^{4}/_{3}$. The area reading is corrected by multiplying by ${}^{16}/_{9}$, the square of the inverted scale.

If the moment disc goes backward, the final reading has to be subtracted from one and the center of the figure is on the side of the axis away from the track, otherwise it is on the same side as the track.

The displacement in the inclined position is of course the same as when erect. An inclined water line is drawn which it is estimated will cut off the right displacement and the displacement to this line determined. The displacement will be in error by the amount of a slice whose thickness is equal to amount of the excess or deficiency in displacement to the heeled water line divided by the area of the water line, which is found by measuring the widths of the water line on each station and applying the trapezoidal rule. With this correction, a new water line is drawn parallel to the trial line, which will cut off nearly the right displacement and the stability for the portion below this line worked out.

It is sufficient in general to determine the stability for a constant displacement as the changes in flotation due to consumption of stores, etc., are very slight, especially in sailing yachts. In large, ocean-going steam yachts, however, considerable changes in displacement may occur on a voyage due to consumption of stores and coal, and it is advisable to work out in such cases the stability at various displacements as well as at various angles of inclination.

If we find the righting arm for several displacements at the same angle of inclination. we may draw what is known as a cross curve of stability, having displacements for abscissæ and righting arms for ordinates. This is the converse of the ordinary curve of stability which has angles of inclination for abscissæ, the displacement remaining constant. A set of cross curves is shown in fig. 19. If we wish to draw an ordinary curve for any given displacement, say 158 tons, we draw an ordinate at that point, and with the values of righting arm for the various angles at this ordinate we draw an ordinary curve, using angles for abscissæ. The cross curves shown in fig. 19 were drawn with an assumed constant position of center of gravity. The center of gravity alters its position, of

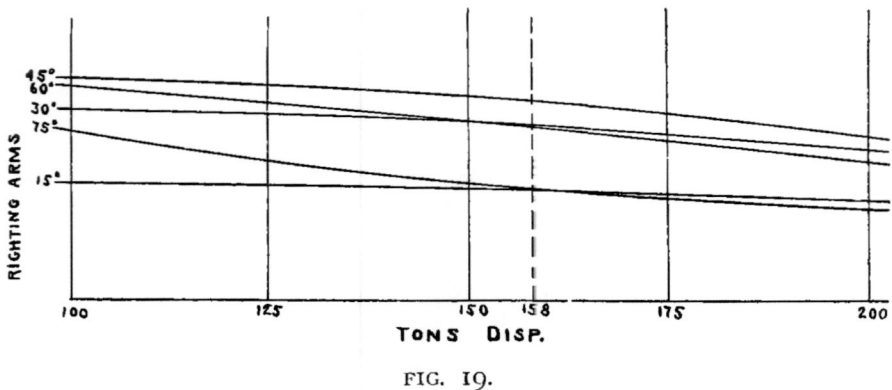

FIG. 19.

course, with a change in loading and displacement and a correction should be made for this as shown on page 42.

The methods of determining stability which have been discussed, assume the yacht to be at rest and in still water. These conditions are of course absent when a yacht is under sail and the actual stability will in general, be greater than the calculated, due to the support afforded by waves at bow and stern. This difference is very great in the case of racing boats with long and low overhangs. For this reason stability work on modern yachts must be considered comparative rather than quantitative, that is, data obtained on sail-carrying power for a given type of boat should be used only for work on boats of that type. For instance, we may wish to know a suitable value for wind pressure for a particular type, in figuring sail area as shown on page 55. Having found the stability for a yacht of the given type having a suitable sail area, assuming the yacht at rest, we may equate the righting and heeling moments as follows: Disp.$\times$arm$=$ A$\times$h$\times$p$\times$cosθ. A is the sail area, h is the vertical distance between the centers of effort and lateral resistance, and p the pressure of the wind on one square foot of sail. All the quantities in this equation are known except p which is readily found by solving the equation. In this way values of p may be found for different types, which used in conjunction with the stability determined in the ordinary manner, enable us to apportion the sail area in accordance with the stability. The stability of steam yachts when under way, is very nearly as calculated.

A phenomenon of importance in connection with stability is the fluctuation in apparent or virtual weight of the yacht when among waves of sufficient size to lift her bodily. As the yacht is lifted on a wave it acquires a certain amount of momentum which tends to decrease the dispacement and virtual weight when the wave commences to subside. The virtual weight is a minimum when on a crest, and it is increased correspondingly in the trough. The direct effect of this on the stability is obvious when we remember that stability is the product of weight and righting arm. This variation of stability when among waves, the force of the wind remaining constant, is the chief cause for a yacht's inability to carry the same amount of canvas in rough water as in smooth.

So far we have considered only statical stability. We have next to consider dynamical stability. This is the amount of work expended in heeling the yacht to a given angle. This work is done in raising the center of gravity, depressing the center of buoyancy, wave-making, eddy-making, and in overcoming frictional resistance. The last three items increase with rapidity of motion and are of slight importance for slow inclinations. The curve of dynamical stability is the integral of the curve of statical stability; that is, the dynamical stability at a certain angle is equal to the area of the curve of righting moments up to that point. Thus we see that the area as well as the shape of the curve of righting moments is of importance.

The period of oscillation is the time consumed in swinging from an inclined position to the opposite position under the influence of the stability. It is expressed theoretically by the following formula:

$$T = .554 \sqrt{\frac{R^2}{GM}}$$

R is the radius of gyration and GM the metacentric height. It will be seen that T varies as the radius of gyration and inversely as the square root of the metacentric height.

The period of oscillation has a very important bearing on the question of speed, as it depends both on the form and the amount and distribution of the weight. as will be seen from the formula. It appears to be of advantage to make the radius of gyration as large as practicable for transverse inclination, and as small as possible for longitudinal inclinations. This is accomplished by spreading the weights transversely and concentrating them amidships longitudinally, thus increasing the radius of gyration and the value of T. This is the reason for "winging out" the ballast in shoal, centerboard boats. The radius of gyration is increased without affecting the metacentric height. Transverse distribution of ballast is not possible in boats having outside ballast.

As we have seen, the total stability is made up of the stability due to form and that due to weight. Now for any given ratio of ballast to displacement, there is probably a certain combination of stability of form and weight more effective for speed under ordinary conditions than any other. This is one of the fundamental principles of yacht design and is, moreover, one of the least understood. The proportion of stability due to weight to the total varies in the same direction as the ratio of ballast to displacement. There is absolutely no data as to what this proportion should be for varying ratios of ballast to displacement. Scientific experimentation along this line would be very difficult, if not impossible, but the results would be of immence value to a skillful designer. A faulty distribution of stability between form and weight is responsible for the failure of many racing yachts, the error being generally in giving too large a proportion of stability to weight, that is, in placing the ballast too low.

A knowledge of the longitudinal and transverse metacentric heights is of value in determining the change of trim or inclination consequent upon moving a weight from one portion of the yacht to another. The moment to change trim one inch is equal to

$$\frac{D \times G\,M}{12 \times L} \text{ foot pounds or foot tons.}$$

D is the amount of the displacement in pounds or tons, GM **the metacentric height or distance from the center of gravity to the longitudinal metacenter, and L is the water-line length in feet. The change of trim is taken as the sum of the amounts by which the boat sinks at the stern and rises at the bow, or vice versa. The longitudinal GM for the thirty-footer is 29.29 ft. The moment to change trim is then

$$\frac{24200 \times 29.29}{12 \times 30} = 1969 \text{ ft. pounds.}$$

Suppose we wish to determine the change in trim due to moving a 100-lb. anchor from the bows to the lazarette, a distance of about 29.5 feet. The moment of the weight of the anchor is then $100 \times 29.5 = 2950$ ft. lbs., and the change of trim is

$$\frac{2950}{1969} = 1.5 \text{ inches.}$$

The longitudinal metacentric height is approximately the same as the water-line length, so that for rough calculations the moment to change trim one inch may be taken as one-twelfth the displacement.
The moment to produce one degree heel is equal to $.01745 \times D \times GM$, where GM is the transverse metacentric height and D the displacement.

For the thirty-footer this moment is $.01745 \times 24200 \times 4.36 = 1841$ ft. lbs.

A boat weighing 150 lbs. would be about 8 feet outboard if carried on davits and would produce a heeling moment of $150 \times 8 = 1200$ lbs. The angle of heel produced would be

$$\frac{1200}{1841} = .65°$$

CHAPTER VII.

BALLAST.

THE function of ballast is to increase the stability due to weight. This is done by increasing the displacement and by increasing the meta-centric height GM through a lowering of G. The proper ballasting of a yacht is of vital importance. With cruising boats, considerations of safety and ability demand a liberal amount of ballast. Where speed alone is the only consideration, however, it is desirable to reduce the amount of ballast to a minimum, the sail-carrying power being furnished by increased stability of form and by the weight of crew. The nice adjustment of stability of form and of weight, according to type as discussed in the chapter on stability is of great importance in all cases.

Lead is more commonly used for ballast than any other material on account of its high density. Its use permits of great concentration and lowering of weight and consequent increase in weight stability. Excess in this direction, however, is a common error. Lead has the further advantage over iron of being uninjured by the action of water. Iron, on the other hand, is much cheaper than lead and may be incorporated in the arrangement for longitudinal strength. Certain types of boats, notably centerboard boats, requiring a considerable amount of inside ballast, perform better with stone or iron ballast than with lead. An explanation of this is that the stone and iron being of smaller density than lead, are of greater bulk for equal weights, thus raising the center of gravity and distributing the weight so as to afford a better combination of stability of form and of weight, and a more suitable value for transverse time of oscillation than would result if lead were used. Transverse distribution and longitudinal concentration of ballast are to be sought in general.

A convenient method of comparison of the weight of ballast carried in different types is by the ratio of ballast to displacement. This ratio for keel cruising boats should lie between .40 and .55. For the semi-keel type the ratio should lie between .30 and .45, being generally in the vicinity of .40. Centerboard cruising boats with inside ballast should have a ratio of from .25 to .40, the ratio lying most commonly between .30 and .35. It is impossible to state any values of this ratio for racing boats, as the amount of ballast is dependent upon the rule under which the boat is built, and varies from zero in the classes with little or no restrictions up to the values stated for cruising boats in classes where the restrictions are more stringent. The ratio ballast to displacement for the thirty-footer is .405.

In all cases it is well to provide for the carrying of a small portion at least, of the ballast inside the boat. Boats carrying all inside ballast are found to require considerable experimentation as to position and distribution of ballast before securing the best results. From this it seems altogether likely than many racing boats with all outside ballast are not sailing in their best form on account of the ballast not being in the most suitable position longitudinally or vertically, particularly the latter. It is difficult to experiment with the vertical position of the ballast but the longitudinal position and resultant trim is readily varied if some inside ballast be carried.

In designs where the entire amount of ballast is to be carried on the keel, it is necessary to make very careful computations for weight and position of center of gravity if accurate results are to be expected. To do this the weight and center of each item entering into the structure and equipment of the yacht must be ascertained. The methods of computing the weights of the various members have been given in chapter II. Care must be taken that nothing be omitted from this calculation. Longitudinal moments must be taken about a convenient axis, usually the midship section so that the position of the center of gravity may be calculated. The distance from the center of gravity of each member to the midship section, multiplied by its weight gives the moment. The moments of weights forward of the midship section are summed up separately from those aft and the difference between the sums of moments divided by the sum of the weights, gives the distance of the center of gravity of the yacht from the midship section. Now, in order that the boat may trim as designed, the moments of boat and ballast taken about the center of buoyancy must be exactly equal, their weights being on opposite sides of the center of buoyancy. The amount of the ballast is made equal to the displacement minus the sum of the other weights. To illustrate this process the computation for weight and center of gravity of the thirty-footer is given below.

WEIGHTS FORWARD OF STATION 9.

ITEM	WT.	ARM.	MOMENT
Keel	525	7.5	3940
Planking	2182	1.15	2515
Frames	1104	1.15	1270
Deck	1130	.03	34
Deck Beams	277	.03	8
Shelves	114	2.	228
Clamps	133	2.3	306
Stringers	179	2.	358
Floors	350	5.	1750
Plank Fastenings	95	1.15	109
Deck Fastenings	62	.03	2
Other Fastenings	190	.10	19
House Deck	135	1.	135
House Coaming	223	1.8	402
House Beams	67	1.	67
Mast Step	52	9.5	493
Deck Straps	35	10.4	364
Rail	49	2.3	113
Knees	75	1.	75
Breasthook	18	23.	413
Centerboard	170	1.8	306
Bitt	14	19.6	274
Paint	150	1.	150
Cabin Floor	136	2.4	327
Cabin Floor Beams	18	2.4	43
Deck Fittings	50	2.	100
Mast	517	9.5	4910
Bowsprit	46	24.6	1130
Staysail	21	14.3	300
Jib	23	20.	460
Blocks	55	8.	440
Running Rigging	85	9.	765
Standing "	90	11.5	1035
Windlass	50	19.5	973
Anchors	160	19.	3040
Cables	200	18.	3600
Lockers	270	.04	11
Ice Box and Ice	275	9.2	2530
Washbowl	25	4.	100
Water Closet	90	7.7	693
Tanks and water	800	2.7	2160
Galley Fittings	80	6.	480
Pipe Berths	30	13.3	399
Bulkheads	232	1.6	371
Personal Effects	250	1.5	375
	10832		37573

WEIGHTS AFT OF STATION 9.

ITEM	WT.	ARM.	MOMENTS
Deadwood	1820	1.7	3095
Tail-Feather	61	14.5	885
Silk	168	2.4	403
Transom	41	19.8	812
Tie Rods	40	.2	8
Rudder Tube	10	11.8	118
Cockpit Coaming	170	10.6	1800
Steering Gear	30	12.2	366
Mainsail	116	4.	464
Main Boom	171	8.3	1420
Gaff	66	1.	66
Carpet	35	1.2	42
Berths	225	2.1	472
Cushions	15	2.	30
People	600	10.	6000
	3568		15981

Now dividing the difference of the moments by the sum of the weights

$$\frac{37573-15981}{10832+3568}=\frac{21592}{1450}=1.50$$

we have 1.50 feet for the distance, the center of gravity is forward of the midsection. Now the center of buoyancy is 1.58 feet forward of the midsection so that the center of gravity comes .08 feet aft of the center of buoyancy. The weight of the lead will be made equal to the displacement minus the sum of the weights, 24207—14400=9807 or about 9800 lbs. It would be desirable to carry a portion of the ballast inside for trimming, but for purposes of illustration it has all been placed on the keel in this design. The moment of the ballast must of course equal the moment of all the other weights, then

$$9800\times\text{arm}=14400\times.08$$
$$\text{arm}=\frac{14400\times.08}{9800}=.12 \text{ ft.}$$

The center of gravity of the lead must then be .12 feet forward of the center of buoyancy or .20 feet forward of sta. 8½, in order that the boat may trim properly.

The next step is to determine the top of the lead on the design so that it will have the required weight and position. To do this a trial line is drawn and the weight and center of the portion thus cut off is determined. With this as a guide, another line is drawn which is estimated will correct the errors in weight and center of the first trial line. If there is still an error, another trial is made and so on until the correct line is found. The volume of the lead is found in the same manner as the volume of the hull in the calculation for displacement. Keel sections are drawn at frequent intervals, 1.5 feet on plate I, and the areas of these sections are taken with a planimeter. The volume and center are then obtained by the application of the trapezoidal rule. Where there is a slot cut through the keel for a centerboard, the volume of the portion cut out is determined and its moment is subtracted from the total moment. The computation for the thirty-footer is as follows:

STA.	PLAN. READING	ARM.	MOMENT
6	.01	5	.05
6½	.17	4	.68
7	.35	3	1.05
7½	.42	2	.84
8	.44	1	.44
8½	.40	0	3.06
9	.36	1	.36
9½	.32	2	.64
10	.25	3	.75
10½	.19	4	.76
	2.91		2.51

Total weight $= 2.91 \times 2 \times {}^{16}\!/_9 \times 1.5 \times 710 = 11020.$

710 is the weight in pounds of one cubic foot of lead.

Center of gravity $= \dfrac{3.06 - 2.51}{2.91} \times 1.5 = .283$ ft. for'd sta. 8½.

Now the area of the portion cut out by the slot is 5.72 square inches on the drawing or $5.72 \times {}^{16}\!/_9 = 10.17$ sq. ft.
The thickness is two inches or .167 feet. The weight cut out is then 10.17 $\times .167 \times 710 = 1202$ pounds. Its center of profile is .95 feet forward of station 8½. Now taking moments and subtracting

$$11020 \times .283 = 3119$$
$$1202 \times .95 = 1142$$
$$\overline{9818 \times .20 \quad 1977}$$

We get .20 feet for the distance which the center of gravity of the lead is forward of station 8½.

The calculation for longitudinal position of the center of gravity is absolutely necessary when all the ballast is to be carried on the keel, in order that satisfactory results may be assured. The relative positions of the center of buoyancy and of gravity vary so widely in different designs that an estimation of the proper position for the center of the ballast is apt to lead to disappointment. The many cases of faulty trim which are constantly occurring may be attributed to carelessness in this matter.

CHAPTER VIII.

THE simplest method of determining the amount of sail for a new design is by direct comparison with some boat of known performance and of approximately the same type. This is the usual method. As an aid in estimating the sail area, the curve on plate VIII has been drawn, using water-line length as a basis of comparison. The sail areas of a large number of successful yachts were used in constructing this curve, and it may be considered thoroughly representative of modern practice for cruising boats. It was found that no distinction could be made between keel and centerboard boats, especially above twenty feet water line. Using this curve for the thirty-footer we get 1280 square feet as a suitable area.

A method of comparison for sail area is by the ratios of sail area to area of wetted surface, and sail area to area of midsection. The former ratio is generally about 3 though it varies between 2 and 4. The ratio of sail area to area of midsection is used a great deal by French naval architects, and is a very good method of comparison. This ratio should be between 45 and 55 for cruising boats. For the thirty-footer it is 53.2. The ratio of sail area to displacement is also used. Theoretically, the sail area should vary as the two-thirds power of the displacement. Let S_1 and D_1 be the sail area and displacement of a certain boat, and S_2 and D_2, the sail area and displacement of another boat of exactly the same form but of different dimensions; then

$$S_1 : S_2 = D_1^{2/3} : D_2^{2/3} \text{ or } S_2 = \frac{S_1 D_2^{2/3}}{D^{2/3}}$$

The correct procedure, theoretically, is to apportion the sail area in accordance with the stability making the heeling and righting moments equal for a reasonable angle of heel, say, twenty degrees. The righting moment is equal to the displacement times the righting arm for the given angle, as explained in chapter VI, while the heeling moment is equal to the pressure on the sails, or pressure per unit area times the area, multiplied by the vertical distance between the centers of effort and lateral resistance. This distance decreases, of course, as the angle of the heel increases, varying as the cosine of the angle. The pressure of the wind on sails for a good whole-sail breeze is generally considered to be a little over one pound per square foot of area, say 1.15 pounds. This is not the absolute pressure of the wind such as mechanical engineers use in designing structures but a sort of constant, determined as on page 45. The assumptions made here are that the sails are perfectly flat surfaces lying in the central plane of the boat, and that the wind blows in a direction perpendicular to the longitudinal axis of the boat. These conditions are, of course, not realized, and for this reason p must be considered a factor for wind pressure.

Equating the heeling and righting moments at 20 degrees for the 30-footer, we have $A \times 1.15 \times 24.6 \times .94 = 24200 \times 1.41$. 24.6 is the distance in feet between the centers of effort and lateral resistance; .94 is the cosine of 20 degrees; 24200 is the displacement in pounds and 1.41 is the right-

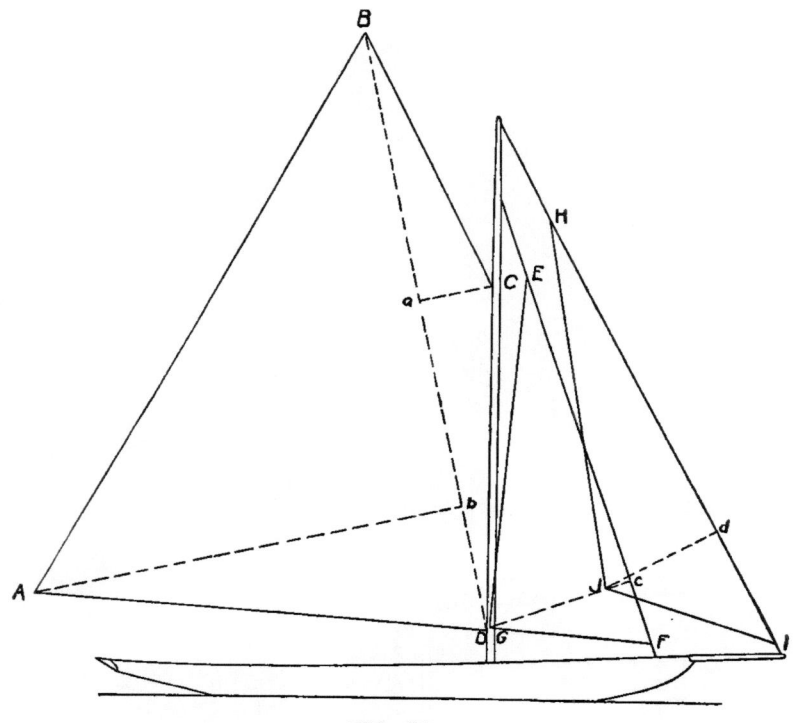

FIG. 20.

ing arm in feet at 20 degrees. Solving the equation we get for the area 1283 square feet.

The area of the sail plan is easily found by dividing it up into triangles and finding the area of each by measuring its base and altitude and taking half the product. Fig. 20 shows the manner in which these measurements were taken on the thirty-footer. The mainsail was divided into the triangles A B D and B C D, A b and a C being the respective altitudes.

The area of the mainsail is then ½BD(Ab+aC). The altitudes of forestaysail and jib are G c and J d and their areas are

$$\text{Forestaysail} = \tfrac{1}{2}\text{E F} \times \text{Gc}$$
$$\text{Jib} \qquad = \tfrac{1}{2}\text{ H I} \times \text{Jd}$$

By the center of effort of a sail plan is generally meant the center of gravity of the areas of all the sails. The true center of pressure is con-

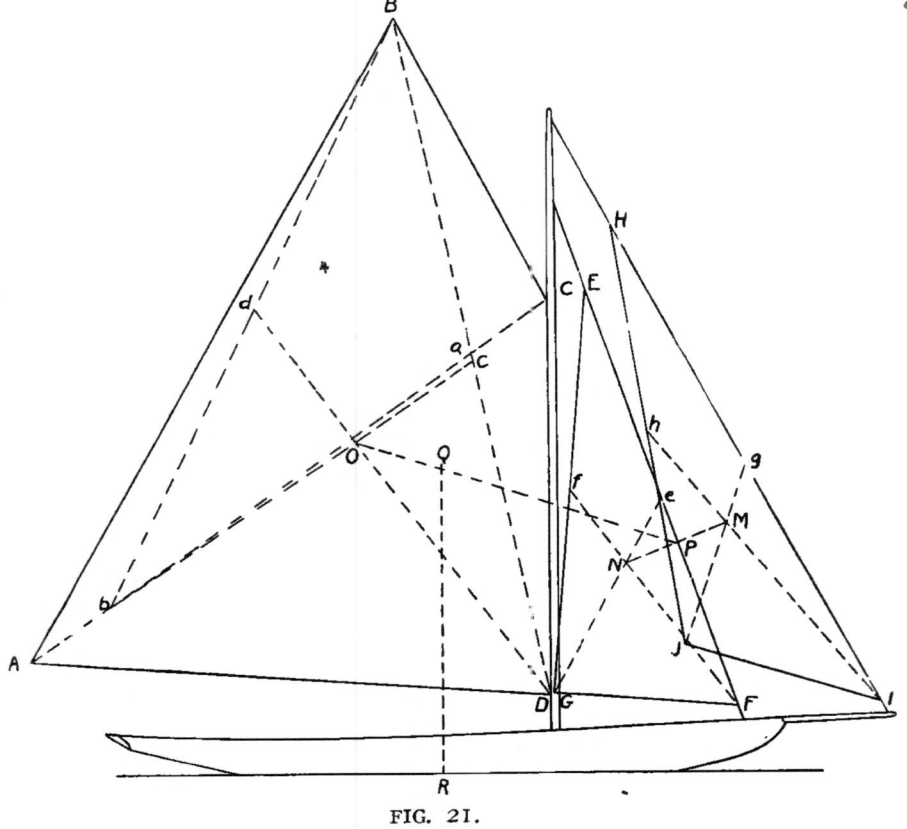

FIG. 21.

siderably ahead of the center of gravity of the sails, and its exact position is impossible to determine. The position of the center of lateral resistance is also impossible to calculate, and as the positions of these two important points are unknown, it is convenient and customary to use instead the center of gravity of the sail plan and the center of lateral plane, the lead being the distance the former is ahead of the latter.

In finding the center of effort, the center of each sail is found and the center of the system is then found by taking moments. Fig. 21 gives the construction for center of effort of the thirty-footer. In finding the center of the mainsail, the second construction given in chapter II for center of a quadrilateral, with no two sides parallel, was used. A b was laid off equal to aC; b B was drawn and bisected, its middle point being at d. Bd was also bisected, its middle point being at c. The center of the sail is at O, the point of intersection of b c and D d. The center of the jib was found by bisecting H I and H J, g and h being the middle points respectively and drawing I h and J G; the center is at M, their point of intersection. The center of the forestaysail, N, was found in a similar manner. The combined center is obtained by finding the center of two sails and then combining with a third, and so on for any number of sails. The areas of the sails for the thirty-footer are, mainsail 934 sq. ft., forestaysail 174 and jib 177. The center of staysail and jib is found at P by taking moments about M thus:

$$MP = \frac{174 \times MN}{174 + 177} = 3.55 \text{ ft.}$$

Now taking the moment of the mainsail about P, we get the center of all three sails at Q, its distance from P being

$$PQ = \frac{934 \times Po}{1285} = 16.8 \text{ ft.}$$

The vertical projection of Q on the water line at R gives a convenient point for locating the fore and aft position of the center of effort.

The proper lead or distance between the centers of effort and lateral plane varies widely with the type of boat. It is conveniently expressed as a fraction of the water-line length. For racing machines of the scow type it varies from 0 to .15, the balance of these boats depending largely on their trim; for shoal, full-ended centerboarders, the lead lies between .05 and .10; for full-ended keel racing boats the lead is generally a little less. For cruising boats of normal form the lead is about .03. In the larger sizes the lead is generally smaller and the center of effort is often placed over and sometimes abaft the center of lateral plane. This is frequently done in the case of catboats for structural reasons, being one of their defects, however. The only way of determining the proper lead is by direct comparison with some well-balanced boat. Even then it is very difficult to get it right in the case of long, full-ended racing boats, and the designer generally resorts to the unscientific device of a movable mast. Many designers neglect the topsails when figuring the center of effort, but it is the opinion of the writer that they should always be included in the calculation, as serious defects in balance have resulted from neglecting them.

The area of sail decided upon has to be subdivided into a number of sails in a manner consistant with ease to handling, appearance, and efficiency. The principal rigs in use to-day are the sloop, schooner and yawl.

The sloop rig is the most efficient, and the yawl the most easily handled. The yawl rig for this reason is becoming more and more commonly used. For the thirty-footer, the double headsail, polemast rig was chosen as being best adapted to this size and type of boat. It is more efficient than the yawl rig and is about as easily handled.

We are very much in the dark as to the most efficient shape of sails. By shape is meant the proportions of the sail and not the amount of flow or draught and general set of the sail. A discussion of the latter would be unprofitable here as it lies within the province of the sailmaker rather than the designer. Every designer has his own theories as to what constitutes an efficient form of sail. Nearly all agree that the forward portion of the sail is the most effective, and that for this reason excessively long booms should be avoided. The relative lengths of head and hoist vary widely with the practice of different designers, some preferring a long hoist with short gaff, while others make head and hoist about equal. The sail should be drawn as it is to be cut, bearing in mind that when the sail is set and fully peaked up, the peak angle or angle between head of sail and axis of mast is from one to three degrees less than that to which the sail is cut. For a boat without a topsail, the peak angle of the mainsail should not be made less than twenty-seven degrees. This is the peak angle to which the mainsail of the thirty-footer is drawn. When topsails are used the peak angle should be about 42 degrees for the mainsail, and 48 degrees for the foresail in schooners. Low booms and low-cut jibs should be avoided as they are in the way, and are not efficient when the boat is heeled well down. High-pointed jibs are inefficient, as they do not draw well and tend to backwind the mainsail. There should be considerable space between jib and mainsail so as to allow a free passage of wind to the mainsail.

CHAPTER IX.

CONSTRUCTION.

A N intimate acquaintance with methods of construction is imperative to the successful designer, as in many cases the form must be adapted to the method of construction to be employed in building the yacht. This is particularly true of the region of the fin in sailing yachts. Moreover, the designer must be thoroughly familiar with the method of construction to be pursued in building, in order that he may determine what the weights will be and provide sufficient displacement accordingly.

The hull of a yacht, particularly an extreme racing yacht, is subjected to a very complicated system of stresses, among which are those produced by the forces acting on the mast, by the leverage of keel or centerboard, by the impact of waves against the hull, and by the tension of the rigging. The designer must thoroughly understand the nature of these stresses in order to be able to design an efficient structure to withstand them. By an efficient structure is meant one where there is no useless weight, and where each member is carefully proportioned to the work it has to do. As displacement is the principal factor for resistance, the saving of weight is of the highest importance where extreme speed is sought. To save weight systematically, each member entering into the structure of the yacht must be carefully designed for the highest efficiency. This necessitates a thorough knowledge of the physical properties of the various materials used in the construction.

The outer skin is the principal member of the yacht's structure, as it is the realization of the desired form, and is, in a sense, the boat itself. All other members may be regarded as auxiliaries in assisting the skin to maintain its function. The principal member for longitudinal strength is the keel, though the skin, deck, stringers, etc., contribute very materially. The transverse strength is supplied mainly by the frames and deck beams. These are assisted in their work by stringers, clamps, floors and knees.

There are various methods of determining suitable scantlings or sizes of the various members of the yacht's structure. The most natural way is to be guided by the scantlings of an existing yacht of about the desired size and type which has proved itself under service conditions to be strong enough and structurally well proportioned. Racing boats often have their scantlings specified by the rules of the particular class for which they are built. It is theoretically possible to compute the necessary sizes for the principal members, but this method is utterly impracticable for ordinary work on account of the immense amount of mathematical labor involved as well as the uncertainity of the exact nature of the stresses to which the yacht is subjected. Something along this line may be done, however, in the case of large yachts of extreme or unusual proportions. In the case of large cruising yachts, the building rules of one of the classification societies furnish the best guide for the determination of suitable scantlings. These building

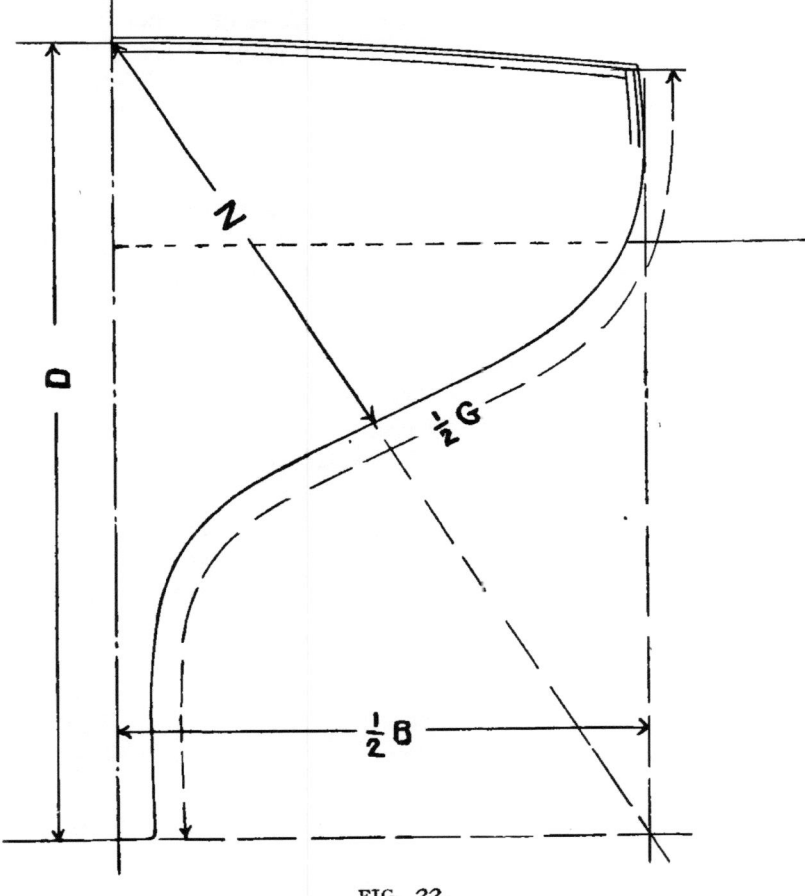

FIG. 22.

rules are based upon the results of practice as well as upon the deductions of scientific research, and may be relied on to produce a substantial and durable hull. It is becoming more common for yachts to be built in accordance with the rules of one of the classification societies, as they may readily be insured if so built, whereas, a yacht independently designed, although possibly superior to one built under the rules, must be completely surveyed before being accepted as a risk.

The classification societies whose rules are most used for yacht construction in this country are Lloyd's Register of Shipping and the American Bureau of Shipping. Lloyd's Register publishes a set of rules especially for yacht construction in steel, composite and wood. These rules are applicable to yachts of all sizes from about twenty feet water line upwards. The scantlings required under these rules are somewhat in excess of those usual to American practice, particularly in the smaller sizes. Under Lloyd's rules the principal scantlings are assigned according to what are known as transverse and longitudinal numbers, which are obtained as shown in figures 22 and 23.

The transverse number is equal to $\frac{1}{2}B+D+\frac{1}{2}G+2N$ (fig. 22), and regulates the sizes of frames and floors. The longitudinal number is equal to the transverse number multiplied by the length obtained as shown in fig. 23.

The longitudinal number regulates the dimensions of planking, keel, stem, sternpost, rudder-stock, shelves and fastenings. The beams are proportioned according to length. The number for equipment is equal to the longitudinal number plus twice the product of the length and height of any erections that may be fitted.

There are three general forms of yacht construction, the all-metal, the all-wood and the composite. These will be dealt with briefly in order. The all-metal construction is the most common for yachts of over eighty feet water line. The advantages of this construction are great strength, durability and increased cabin accommodations. Steel is the usual material used, although aluminum and bronze are sometimes employed, the former on account of its light weight and the latter on account of its smooth surface. It is doubtful whether the smoother surface of bronze compensates for its greater weight as compared with steel.

The midship section of the 100-foot schooner yacht shown in fig. 24, will serve to illustrate the principal features of construction in steel. The sizes of members are expressed as follows: plates in pounds per square foot of area or in twentieths of an inch thickness. A steel plate one inch thick weighs about forty pounds per square foot or two pounds for each

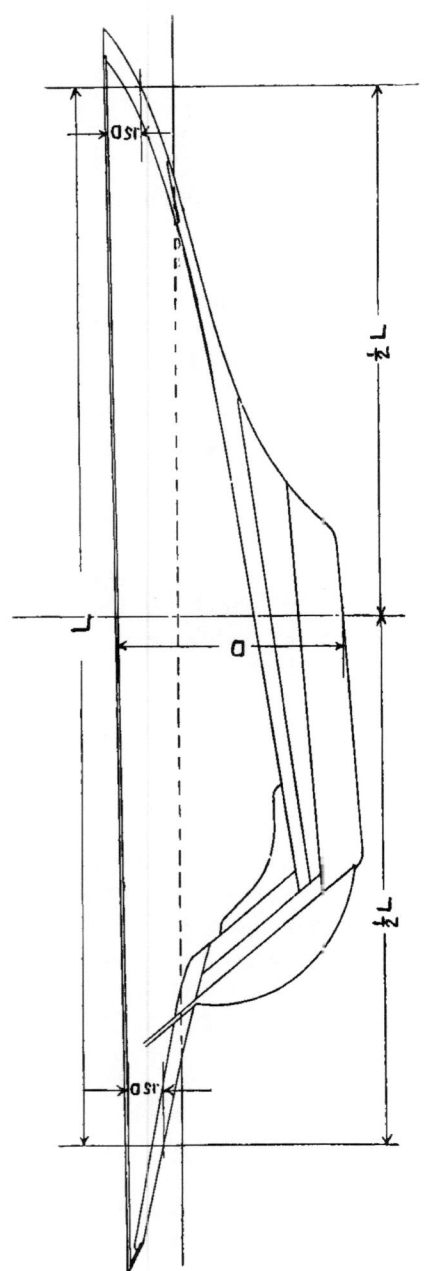

FIG. 23.

twentieth of an inch thickness. Angle bars, I bars, etc., are rated according to the dimensions of their legs, and their weight per lineal foot or thickness in twentieths of an inch.

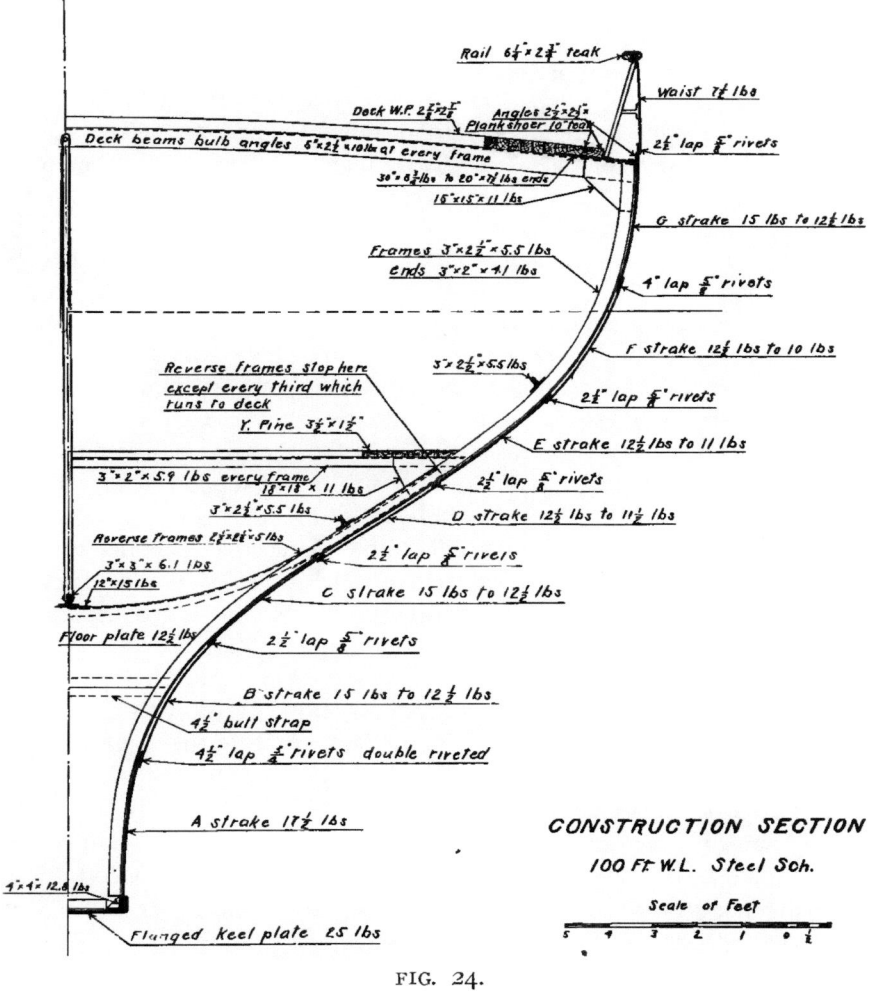

FIG. 24.

The keel of the schooner shown in fig. 24 is a twenty-five pound plate flanged at the sides and riveted to the garboard strake. The latter and the sheer strake are heavier than the remainder of the plating, as they are subjected to greater stresses. The system of plating shown is the ordinary "clencher" or "in and out" style. Flush plating is often used above the water line on yachts for the sake of appearance, but it is heavier, more expensive, and not so strong as the "clencher" system. The frames are steel angles 3"×2½"×5.5 pounds spaced 22" Each pair of frames is' tied together at the feet by floor plates. The keel plate is attached to the floor plate by short angle clips. Deep frames, consisting of plate riveted to ordinary frames, are fitted at the masts to take the strain of the rigging. Angle irons, known as reverse frames, extend across the top of each floor plate and are riveted to the backs of the frames. These tie the frames together very securely and stiffen the floor plate. The keelson shown consists of a flat plate and two angles riveted together. The deck beams are bulb angles and are supported in the middle by steel pillars. They are attached to the frames by bracket plates. The brackets are often welded on the beam itself.

A deck stringer plate is worked all around the vessel between the beams and the wood deck. This is connected with the sheer strake by an angle bar as shown. Another angle some ten inches inboard and parallel to the deck line is riveted to the stringer plate, and the space between the two angles forms a waterway to drain water to the scuppers. The bulwarks are of 7½-pound plating, riveted to sheer strake and supported at frequent intervals by stanchions. They should be capped by a broad teak rail. The deck is of white pine plank laid parallel to the centerline and bolted to deck beams. The bilge stringers consist of a pair of angles riveted back to back. Steel plates are fitted at each mast beneath the wood deck, and these are connected with the deck stringer plate by diagonal tie plates to take the strain of masts and prevent the deck from wringing.

The ballast is lead stowed inside the fin and covered with a layer of cement. Limber holes are cut through the floor plates at the surface of the cement to allow bilge water to drain to the lowest point.

The all-wood construction is almost universal in this country for yachts of less than fifty feet water line. Plate II is the construction plan of the thirty-footer and may be taken as typical of construction in wood. The following paragraphs are descriptive of the various members and of the customary materials with their relative values.

Planking—The woods commonly used for planking of yachts are yellow or hard pine, cedar, white pine, Spanish cedar and mahogany. Other woods such as cypress and oak are occasionally used, but they are less suitable than those first mentioned. Yellow pine is a tough, durable wool and is obtainable in very long lengths. It is quite a heavy wood and for that reason its use is confined to cruising boats. Cedar is a light, easily-worked wood and does not absorb water badly. It is obtainable in short lengths only, which necessitates a large number of butts in a boat of any length. White pine resembles cedar very much, but is less durable. It is used largely for the inner skin of double-planked boats. Spanish cedar and mahogany are quite extensively used for planking, especially on racing boats, although they are considerably heavier than cedar. Their use is partly on account of their handsome appearance when finished bright, but more especially because they stay in place and retain a smooth finish better than other woods. Double planking is now quite extensively used on expensively built boats. The advantages claimed for double planking are greater strength and less liability of leaking, less weight, and a smoother surface. The last point is the only advantage at all marked, the others being doubtful. The best method of double planking is to make the inner skin nearly as thick as the outer, neither skin being calked. Watertightness is secured by applying white lead very thickly between the skins. This acts as a cement, binding the two skins together and squeezing out through the seams renders them watertight. Calking is unnecessary and prevents the surface being as smooth as it otherwise would be. In fastening double planking the inner skin is first tacked in place, and then both skins are through fastened to the frames. Between the frames the inner skin should be fastened to the outer with brass screws. The principal types of fastenings used for planking are copper nails riveted on burrs, brass screws, chisel-point galvanized-wire nails, and galvanized-cut nails. Their value as fastenings stands about in the order given.

Frames—Oak is the usual material for frames, although American elm and hackmatack are admirably adapted to the purpose. Frames are of two kinds, steam-bent and sawed. Steam-bent frames are lighter for the same strength and are used in yachts up to about thirty feet water line. Where bent frames are used, the form of the boat is determined by moulds made from the design enlarged to full size in the mould loft. These are erected in their proper places on the keel, being spaced from two to four feet apart. After a sufficient number of ribbands have been fastened to the moulds, the frames may be put in hot, fastening them against the ribbands where they cool in shape. The bevel is obtained by putting a twist in the frame. Some builders bend their frames around moulds to a little greater curvature than they will have in the boat, and after they have dried they are cut to the proper bevel and put into the boat cold. This method entails more labor than the first. In small craft with little deadrise the frames may be made continuous from rail to rail. Where the frames are separate on each side, as is generally the case, the strength at the centerline must be preserved by connections known as floors. Frames larger than two inches square cannot be bent readily.

Where frames are too large to bend, the sawed frame construction is used. Each frame is usually double and is built up of several short lengths from natural crooks sawed to shape. These short lengths "break joints" on the two halves of the frame, thus preserving the strength. The usual practice is to use all sawed frames in yachts over forty feet. In yachts between twenty-five and forty feet water line a combination of sawed and bent frames is commonly used, every other or every third frame being sawed. This system of framing is used on the thirty-footer (see plate II). With this method the boat is ribbanded up on the sawed frames, the bent frames being put in in the usual way.

Keel—Keels are generally made from oak, though where a boat is to remain in the water most of the time, maple is much better. Elm, beech and birch also make good keels. Keels are of various styles, according to the type of boat. Fig. 25 shows the construction of a small, shoal centerboard boat. Here there is no keel proper, the longitudinal strength being furnished by keelsons notched over the frames which are continuous from rail to rail, fore and aft of the box. The port bedlog extends aft for a keelson, while both bedlogs are through fastened to the forward keelson, which is on the centerline. Fig. 26 shows a somewhat similar construction for a small keel boat. Here all the frames are continuous and the keelsons extend inboard far enough to get a good fastening into the deadwood. The strength amidships is furnished by the deadwood. The construction of a larger keel boat is illustrated by fig. 23. All the frames box into the keel, and transverse strength at the centerline is preserved by floors at frequent intervals. The keel is deep enough to furnish the necessary longitudinal strength without a keelson. Another style of keel is that of the thirty-footer shown on plate II.

Stringers etc.—Stringers, shelf and clamp are usually of yellow pine. Oak is sometimes used and spruce where especial lightness is desired.

Deck—White pine is almost universally used for decks. Where it is finished bright the seams are payed with some elastic seam composition after being calked. Yachts with a house generally have the deck planks sprung parallel with the planksheer. Where a yacht is flush-decked or has a house running straight fore and aft, like the thirty-footer, the deck planks usually run straight, as this makes a little more shipshape appearance. Canvas-covered decks are used a great deal for small yachts, as a tight deck is thus secured with a thinner planking than could be used otherwise. The deck planks should be matched boards of most any light wood.

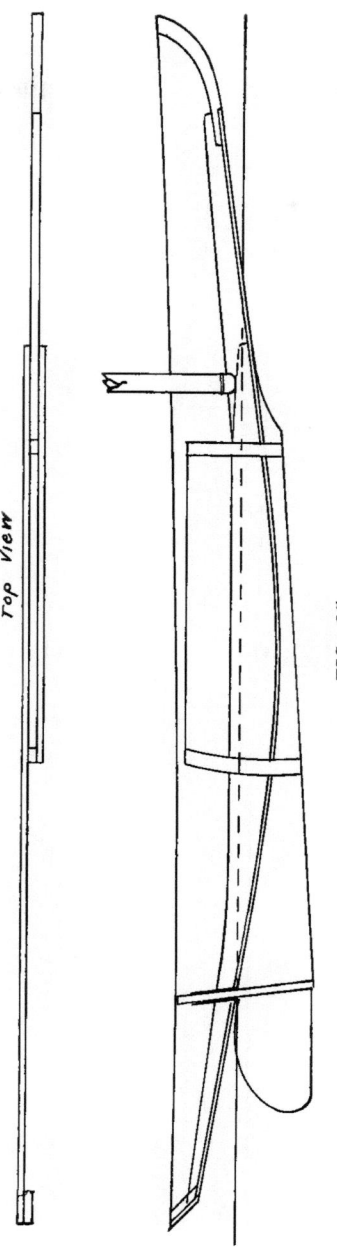

TOP VIEW

FIG. 25.

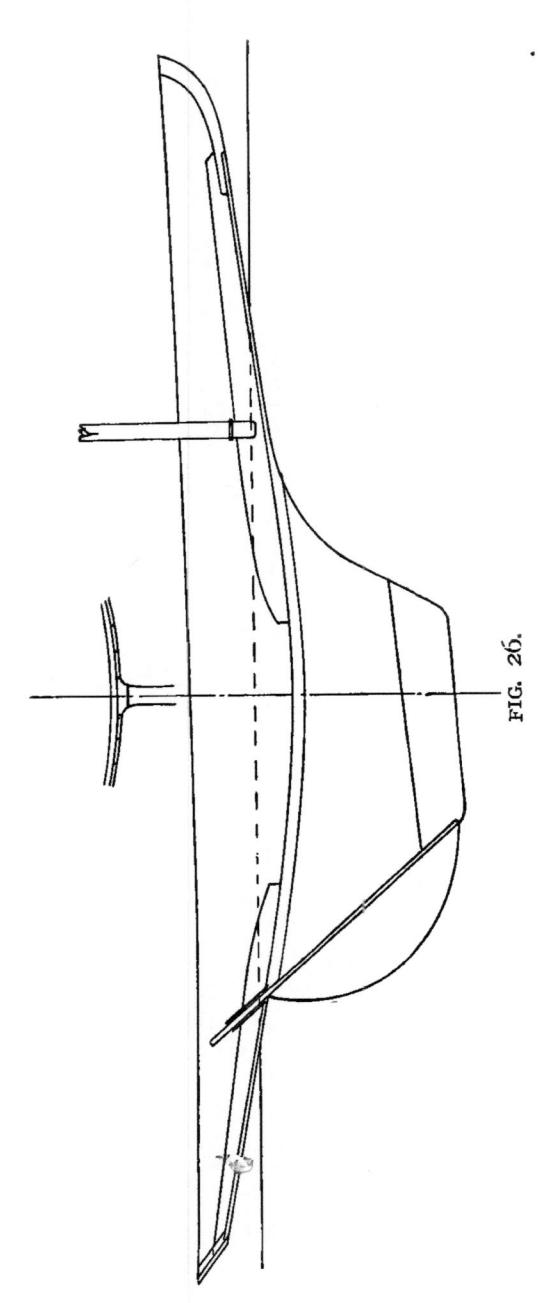

FIG. 26.

Deck Beams—Oak is commonly used for deck beams, though spruce may be used where extreme lightness is a desideratum. Beams are sawed to shape unless the crown is excessive, when they must be steamed and bent. Extra heavy beams should be located at masts, at ends of house and cockpit, and at skylights on other deck openings. These are termed main beams. Other intermediate beams continuous across the boat are called auxiliary beams, and the beams along each side of the house are known as half beams.

Miscellaneous—Floors are of oak or galvanized wrought iron. Bronze keel bolts should not land on iron floors, as galvanic action is liable to occur. Keel bolts are generally of Tobin or other strong bronzes, which have an elastic limit of about 30000 pounds. The lower end is commonly enlarged by forging to hold the lead, but it is better practice to thread and nut both ends, as forging reduces the strength of bronze. Lloyd's Register gives very complete rules for the determination of sizes of keel bolts based on width, depth and sectional area of the lead and on the spacing of the bolts. Customary working loads for various diameters of bolt are given roughly in the following table.

DIAMETER	$\frac{1}{2}''$	$\frac{5}{8}''$	$\frac{3}{4}''$	$\frac{7}{8}''$	$1''$	$1\frac{1}{8}''$	$1\frac{1}{4}''$	$1\frac{3}{8}''$	$1\frac{1}{2}''$
Load per bolt, lbs.	200	300	440	600	790	990	1230	1480	1770

Knees and stem are of natural crook oak or hackmatack. Tie rods and deck straps as shown on plate II, are very effective. The tie rods at mast communicate a portion of the thrust of the mast to the main beams thus relieving the keel. The deck straps are let into the beams and are well fastened to deck plank and beams. They resist the wringing tendency of the mast.

The foregoing covers very briefly the principal points of construction in wood. Table VIII gives a representative schedule of scantlings for cruising boats of various water-line lengths. The weights of various woods are given in table II.

The composite construction is a combination of the all-wood and all-metal construction and is used largely on yachts of from fifty to ninety feet water line. With this construction the frames, floors, reverse frames, keelson, stringers and deck beams are of steel, while the keel, planking and deck are of wood. Sometimes a part of the frames and deck beams are of wood also. Fig. 27 is the midship section of a seventy-five-foot schooner and is typical of the composite construction. A flanged steel plate is bolted on top of the wood keel and to this the frames are riveted. Floor plates, clips and reverse frames complete the strength at the centerline.

The wood keel is of maple nine inches thick. The lead is cast in one piece and the bolts pass through the keel and set up on the inside of keel plate. Other features are similar to the all-metal construction.

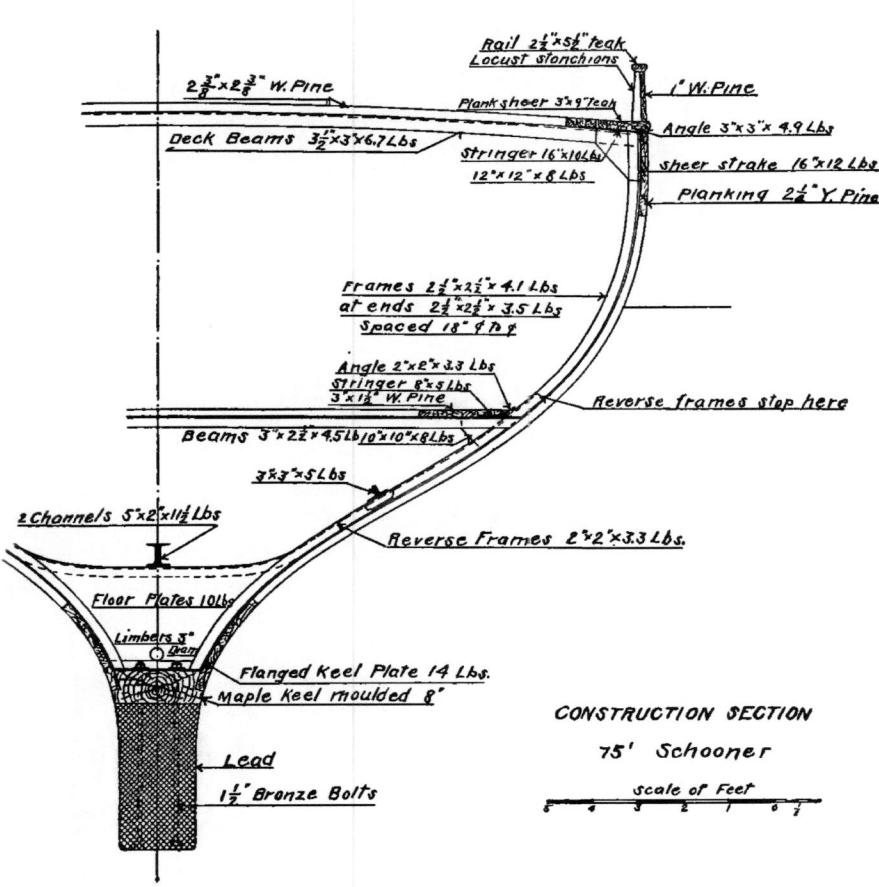

FIG. 27.

APPENDIX

DATA ON THIRTY-FOOT W. L. CRUISER.

Length O. A. ....45' 9"
  " L. W. L. ....30' 0"
Beam Extreme. ....12" 0'
  " L. W. L. ....11' 7"
Draught Extreme. ....5' 2½'
  "   to Centerline. ....2' 11"
Overhang For'd. ....7' 0"
  "   Aft. ....8' 9"
Freeboard For'd. ....3' 7"
  "   Aft. ....2' 8"
  "   Least. ....2' 5"
Area of Midship Section. ....24.2 Sq. Ft.
  " " Lateral Plane (Board down). ....112.6 " "
  " " L. W. L " ....245.2 " "
  " " Wetted Surface (Board down). ....402.6 " "
  " " Sails total. ....1285 " "
  " " Rudder ....12.4 " "
Displacement Above Centerline. ....20800 Lbs.
  "   Below   " ....3407 "
  "   Total. ....24207 "
C. B. from For'd End L. W. L. ....16.42' 54.8% L. W. L.
C. E. " " " " ....16.15' 53.8 " "
C. G. L. " " " " ....16.30' 54.4 " "
C. L. P. " " " " ....17.04' 56.8 " "
Prismatic Coefficient (using total Midship Section). 522
L. W. L.   " 705
Lbs. per Inch Immersion at L. W. L. 1307
Ratio Ballast to Displacement. 405
  " Sail Area to Area Midship Section. 53.2
  " Lateral Plane to Area Midship Section. 4.65
  " Rudder to Lateral Plane. 110
Weight of Hull. ....10800 Lbs.
  " " Rig. ....1200 "
  " " Crew. ....600 "
  " " Ballast. ....9800 "
  " " Equipment. ....1800 "

TABLE I

NATURAL TANGENTS AND CORRESPONDING SECANTS.

TANGENT	SECANT	TANGENT	SECANT	TANGENT	SECANT	TANGENT	SECANT
.010	1.000	.160	1.013	.310	1.047	.460	1.101
.020	1.000	.170	1.014	.320	1.050	.470	1.106
.030	1.000	.180	1.016	.330	1.053	.480	1.109
.040	1.001	.190	1.018	.340	1.056	.490	1.114
.050	1.001	.200	1.020	.350	1.060	.500	1.118
.060	1.002	.210	1.022	.360	1.063	.510	1.123
.070	1.002	.220	1 024	.370	1.066	.520	1.127
.080	1.003	.230	1.026	.380	1.070	.530	1.132
.090	1.004	.240	1.028	.390	1.073	.540	1.137
.100	1.005	.250	1.031	.400	1.077	.550	1.141
.110	1.006	.260	1.033	.410	1.081	.560	1.146
.120	1.007	.270	1.036	.420	1.085	.570	1.151
.130	1.008	.280	1.038	.430	1.089	.580	1.156
.140	1.010	.290	1.041	.440	1.093	.590	1.161
.150	1.011	.300	1.044	.450	1.097	.600	1.166

TABLE II

WEIGHT OF A CUBIC FOOT OF SUBSTANCES.

NAME OF SUBSTANCE	AVERAGE WEIGHT POUNDS
Aluminum	162
Anthracite	54
Ash	40
Birch	40
Bronze	525
Butternut	35
Cedar, white or red dry 30, soaked	40
" Spanish	35
Cement	55
Copper rolled	548
Elm	35
Gasoline	42
Hackmatack	35
Iron, cast	450
" wrought	480
Lead, cast	710
Mahogany	53
Maple	48
Oak dry 50, soaked	56
Pine, Oregon	35
" white	28
" yellow dry 40, soaked	45
Spruce	31
Steel Plates and Shapes	490
Teak	50
Water, fresh	62.4
" salt	64.0

TABLE III

WEIGHTS OF SPRUCE SPARS PER FOOT OF LENGTH

(*For Oregon Pine Multiply by* 1.13)

DIAM.	WT.	DIAM.	WT.	DIAM.	WT.	DIAM.	WT.	DIAM.	WT.
3″	1.62	5¼	4.96	7½	10.10	9¾	17.1	14	35.3
3¼	1.90	5½	5.43	7¾	10.8	10	18.0	14½	37.8
3½	2.20	5¾	5.95	8	11.5	10½	19.8	15	40.5
3¾	2.53	6	6.54	8¼	12.2	11	21.8	15½	43.2
4	2.88	6¼	7.02	8½	13.0	11½	23.8	16	46.0
4¼	3.25	6½	7.60	8¾	13.8	12	25.9	16½	48.8
4½	3.65	6¾	8.20	9	14.6	12½	28.1	17	52.0
4¾	4.07	7	8.82	9¼	15.4	13	30.2	17½	55.0
5	4.50	7¼	9.46	9½	16.2	13½	32.7	18	58.3

TABLE IV.

WEIGHTS OF SAILS IN POUNDS PER 100 SQ. FT. OF AREA.

Cloths 16″ Wide		*Cloths 20″ Wide*	
NO.	WT.	OZ.	WT.
000	26.2	12	14.1
00	24.9	10	12.6
0	23.7	8	11.0
1	22.5		
2	21.2	*Cloths 28½″ Wide*	
3	20.0	7	6.9
4	18.8	6	6.0
5	17.5	5	5.0
6	16.2	4	4.0
7	15.0		
8	13.8		
9	12.6		
10	11.4		

TABLE V

FASTENINGS

NUMBER OF NAILS IN ONE POUND

LENGTH	COPPER NAILS	GALV. BOAT NAILS	GALV. WIRE NAILS
¾"	710	500	800
⅞"	600	450	700
1"	495	400	550
1¼"	320	300	400
1½"	215	200	260
1¾"	155	135	170
2"	115	95	110
2¼"	85	68	80
2½"	65	50	70
3"	44	33	57
3½"	30	24	43
4"	20	20	30

TABLE VI

AREA CURVE FACTORS

	1	2	3	4
P. C.	.507	.519	.530	.557
C. B	52.8%	53.4%	53.9%	55.3%
1	.080	.080	.080	.080
2	.285	.285	.285	.285
3	.560	.560	.560	.560
4	.808	.808	.808	.808
5	.972	.972	.972	.972
6	.978	.983	.983	.988
7	.800	.823	.850	.900
8	.447	.507	.557	.677
9	.138	.167	.200	.296

Mid section 56% of L. W. L. abaft forward point of immersion.

TABLE VII

RATIOS OF RUDDER TO LATERAL PLANE

L. W. L.

20′	.14
25	.12
30	.11
35	.10
40	.095
45	.085
50	.080
60	.070
70	.060
80	.056
90	.052
100	.050

TABLE VIII

REPRESENTATIVE SCANTLINGS IN WOOD FOR KEEL BOATS

L.W.L.	Keel Sided	Stem Sided	Frames Spaced	Frames Sec. Area	Plank Thickness	Deck Thickness	Deck Beams Sec. Area	Shelf & Clamp Sec Area	Stringers Sec. Area
15'	7"	2¾"	8"	.9"	⅝"	¾"	1"	3"	4"
18	8	3	9	1.0	¾	⅞	1.3	4	4
21	9	3¼	10	2.3	⅞	1	1.7	8	6
25	11	3¾	12	3.3	1	1⅛	2.3	12	8
30	13	4¼	12	4.8	1⅛	1¼	3.0	16	10
35	14	5	12	6.0	1¼	1⅜	3.7	20	12
40	15	5½	14	7.7	1⅜	1½	4.4	24	14
45	16	6	16	11.	1½	1⅝	5.1	28	16
50	17	6½	18	14.	1⅝	1¾	6.5	31	18
60	19	7½	22	21.	1⅞	2	13.	37	23
70	21	8	24	28.	2⅛	2¼	19.	43	27
80	23	9	24	36.	2⅜	2⅜	22.	49	31
90	25	9½	24	43.	2⅝	2½	24.	55	35

Deck beams spaced same as frames.

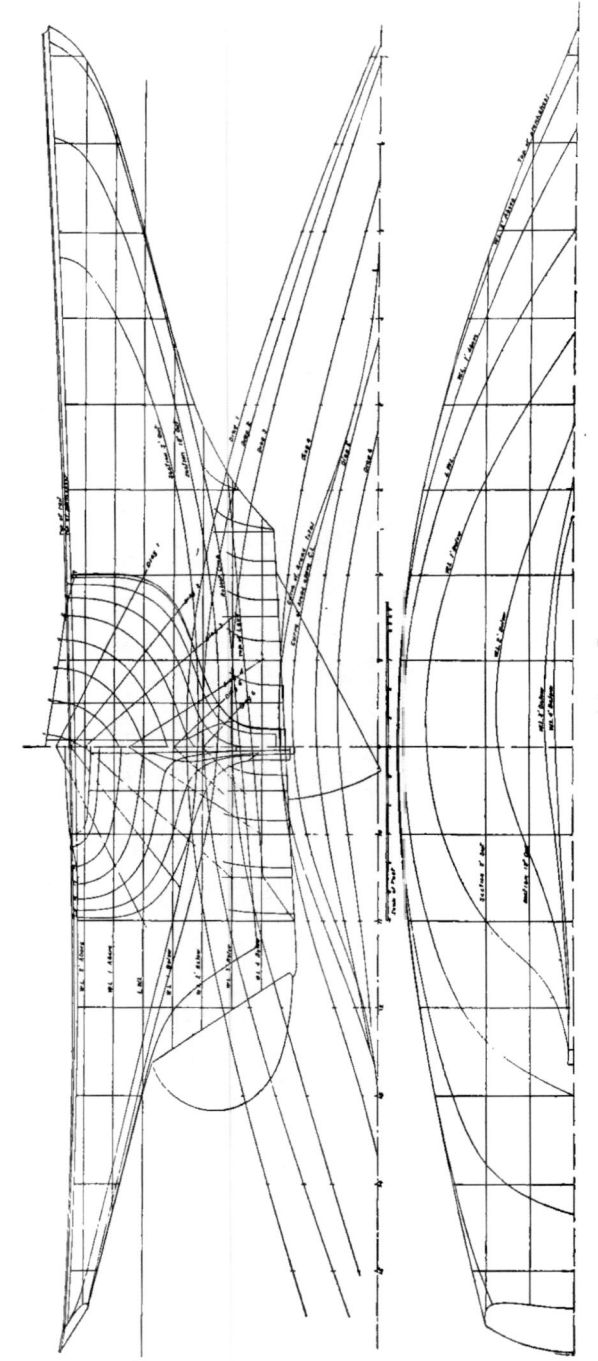

PLATE I.

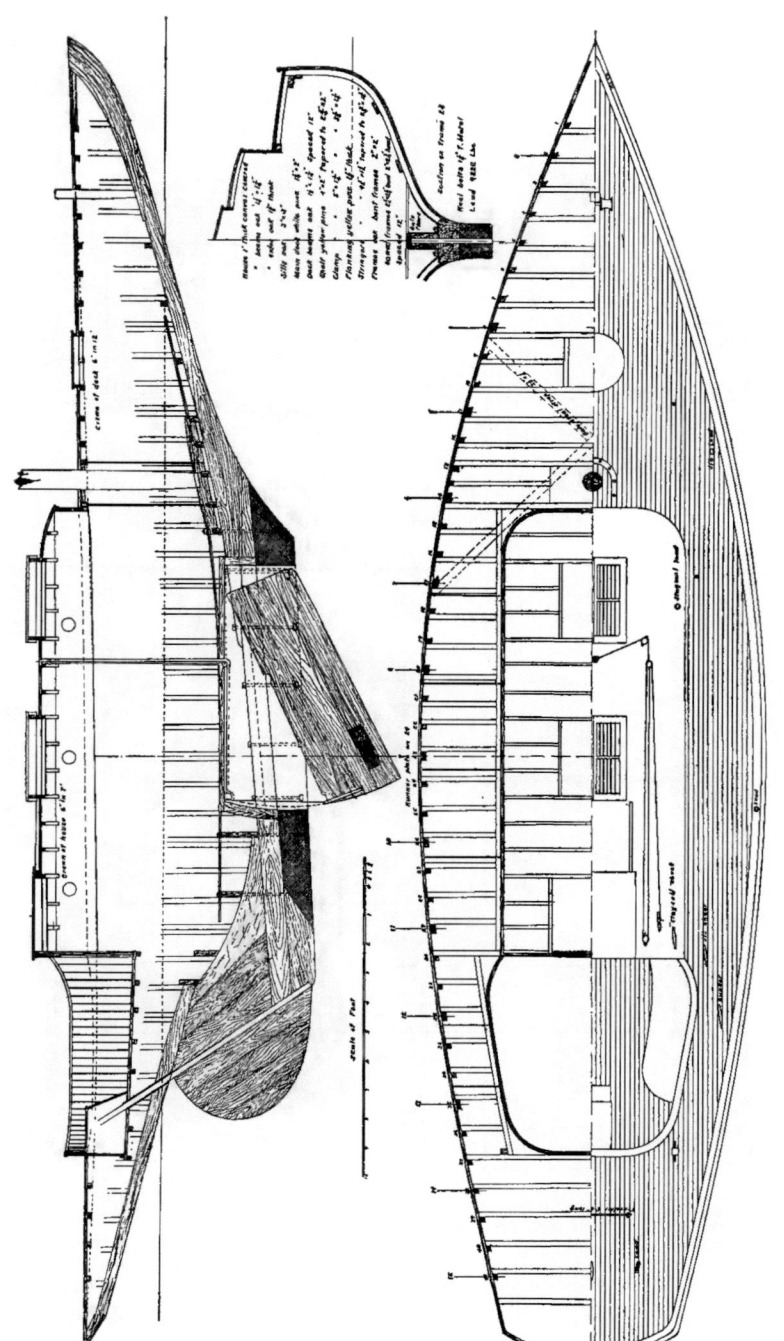

PLATE II.

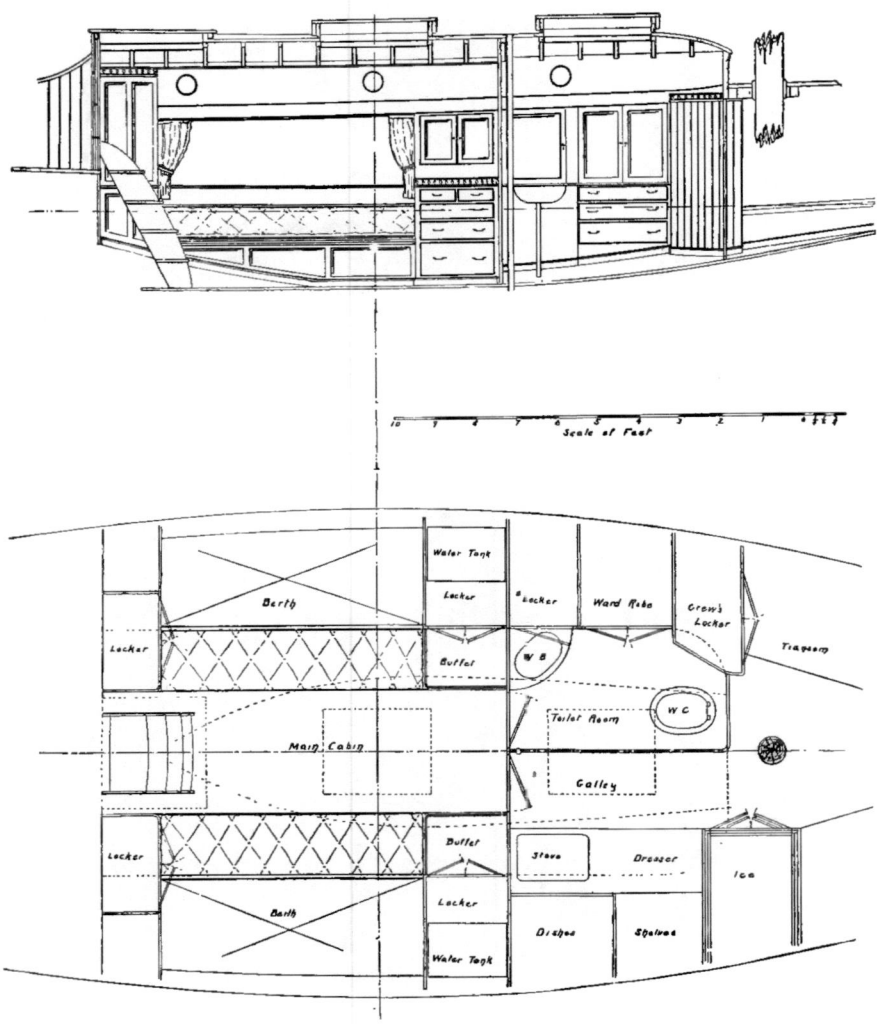

Scale of Feet

PLATE III.

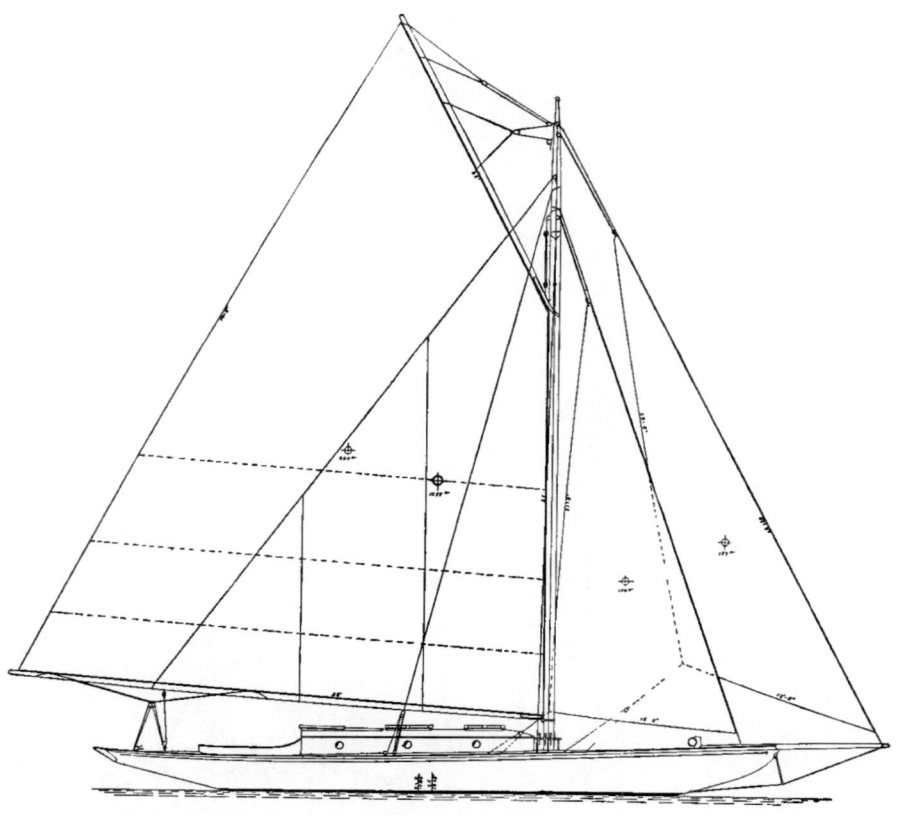

PLATE IV.

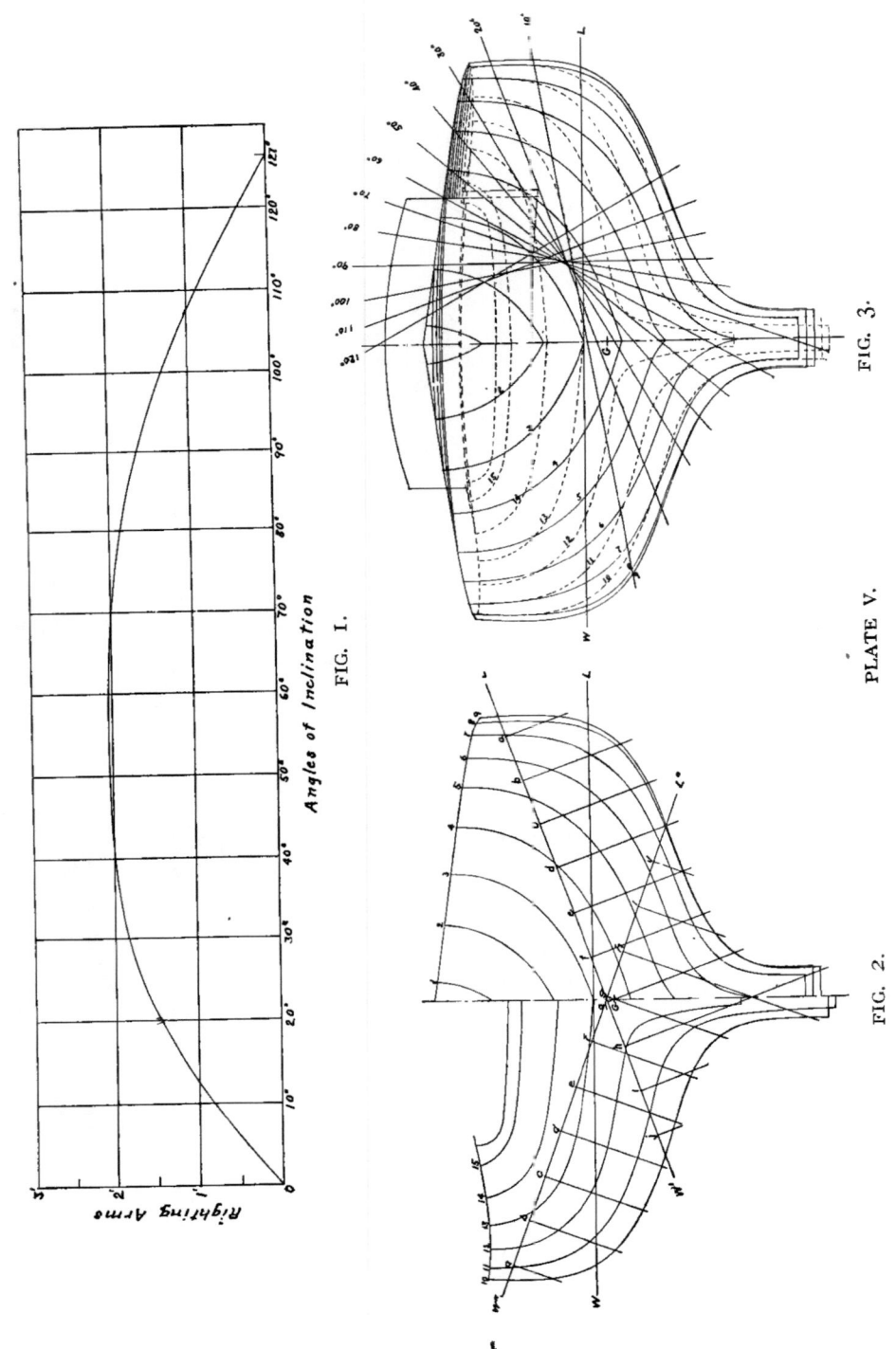

FIG. I.

Angles of Inclination

Righting Arms

FIG. 2.

FIG. 3.

PLATE V.

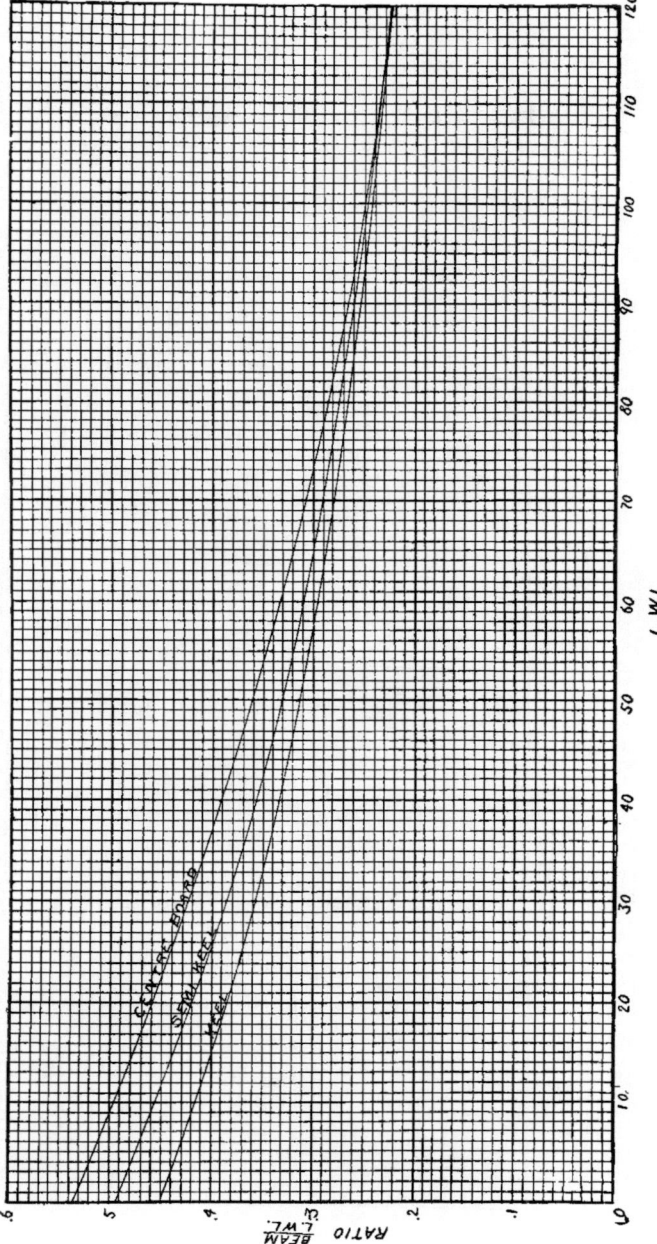

CENTER BOARD

SEMI-KEEL

KEEL

RATIO $\frac{BEAM}{L.W.L.}$

L.W.L.

PLATE VI.

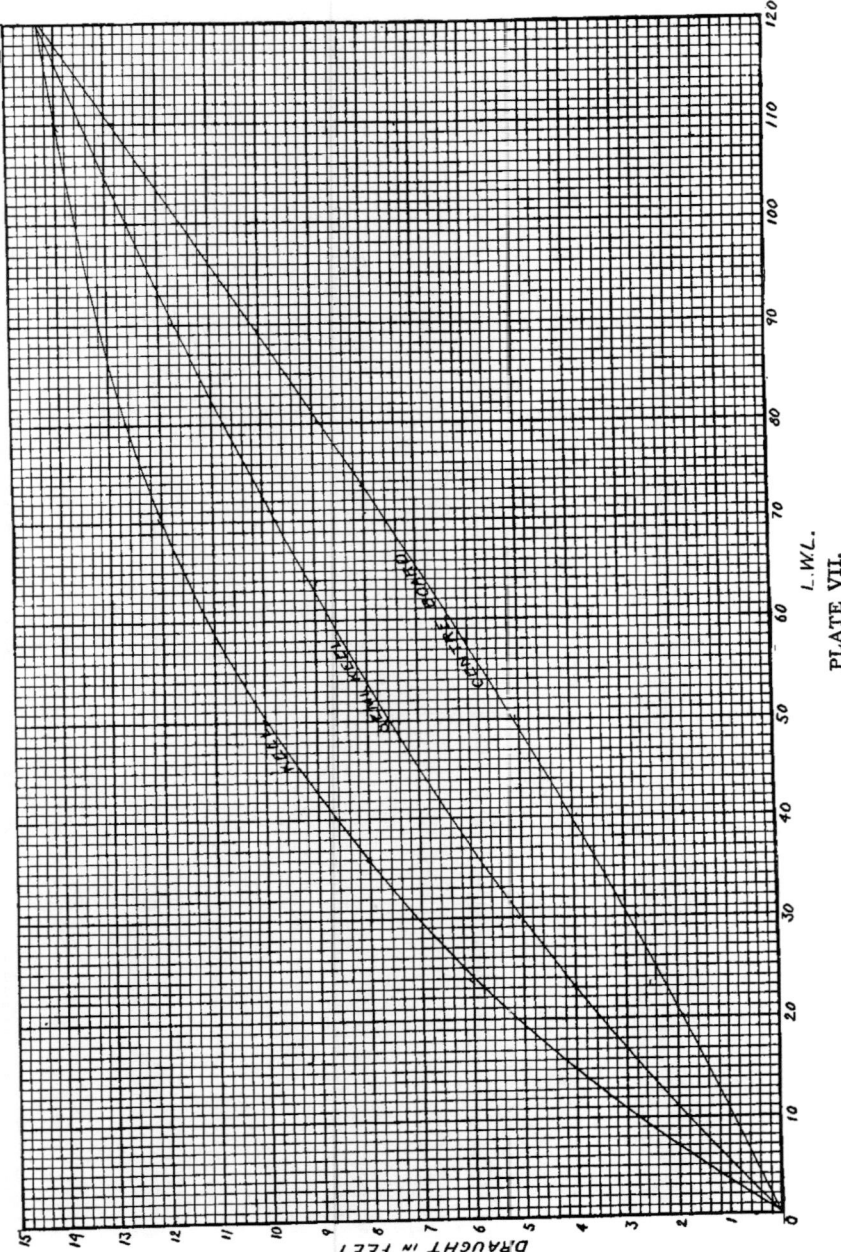

DRAUGHT IN FEET

L.W.L.

PLATE VII.

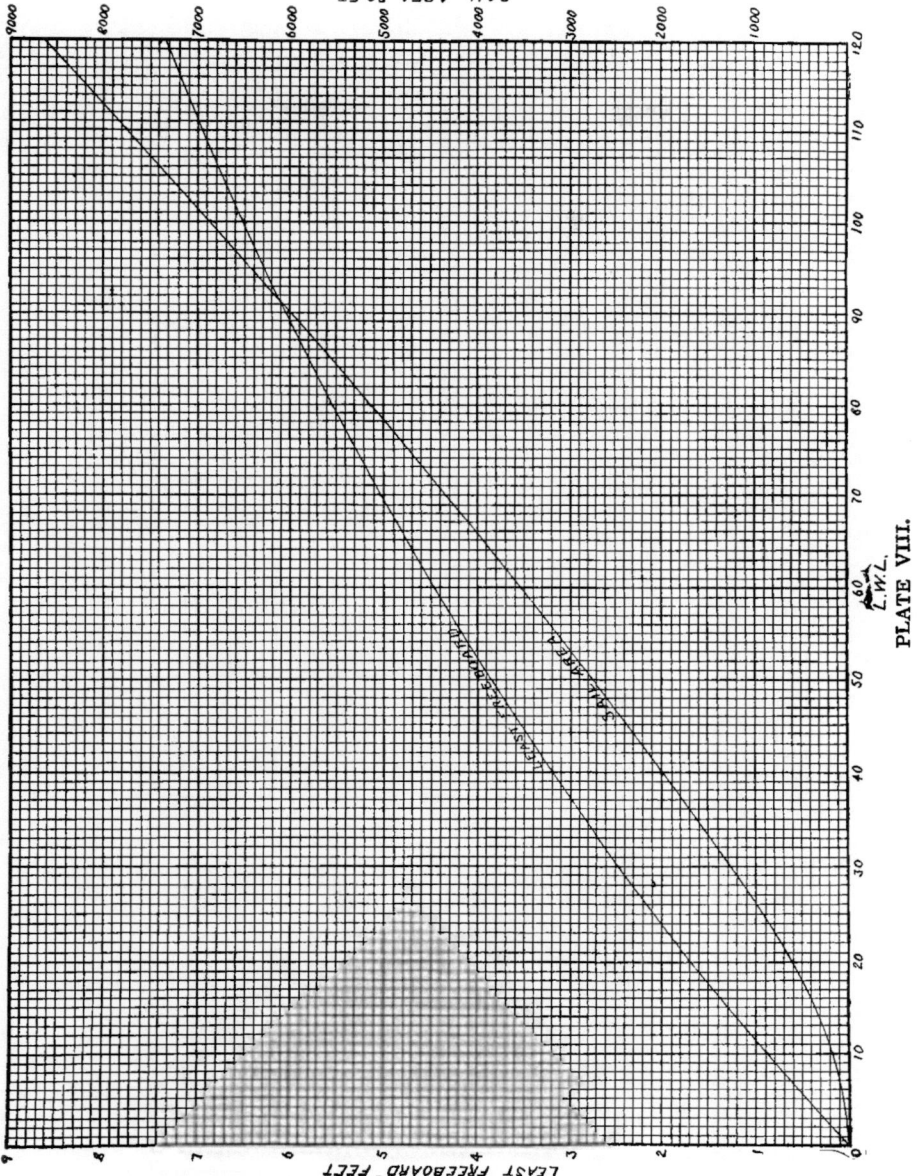

PLATE VIII.

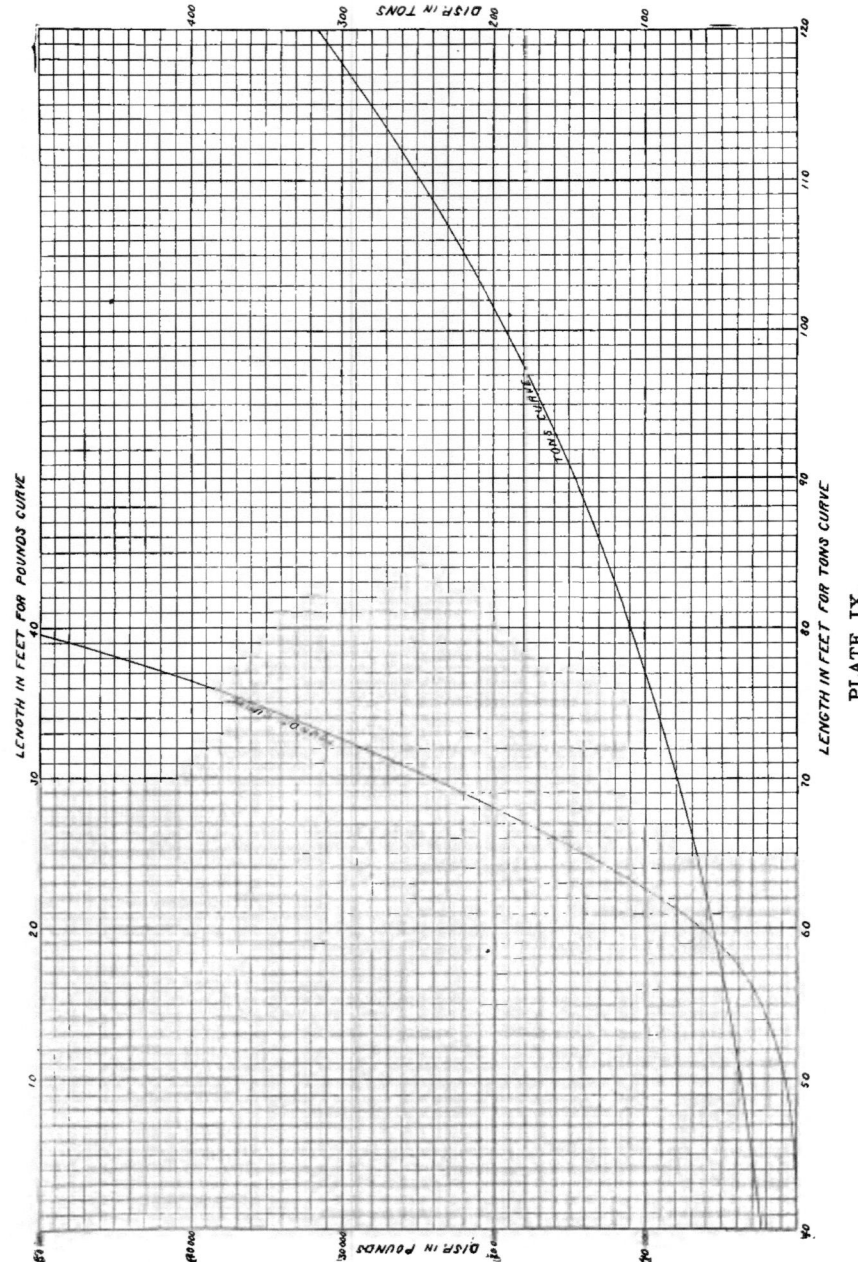

PLATE IX.

INDEX

PAGE

Analysis of righting couple...........33
Areas of plain figures............... 9
Areas of sails......................56
Ballast, amount of..................48
Calculation of weights...............16
Center of buoyancy, fore and aft
    position 19
    vertical position.19
Center of effort.....................56
Center of gravity, plain figures....... 9
    sails 57
    of the yacht.......34
Center of lateral plane..............24
Change of trim due to shifted weight.46
Co-efficient for wind pressure.......55
Composite construction...............69
Correction for change in position of
    C. of G..................42
Cross curves of stability.............44
Curve of areas of transverse sections..18
Curve of righting arms..............38
Determination of proportions.......29
Displacement, calculation of..........19
    determination of amount.19
Dynamical stability..................45
Heel, angle of, due to shifted weight..47
Inclining experiment for finding
    C. of G..................35
Lateral plane, area of...............25
    shape of..............26
Lead of centre of effort.............57
Lines, fairing up process............32
Metacentric height, definition........33
    determination of..37
    suitable values....38
Midship section, area of..............20

Moment of inertia of water line,
    long. axis.......14
  of water line,
    trans. axis......15
Prismatic co-efficient.................20
Resistance, nature of................. 2
Rigs 58
Rudders, size of....................26
Sail area, determination of..........54
Sails, shape of......................58
Scantling, determination of.........60
Simpson's rule...................... 5
Stability, Blom's method.............39
    division of.................46
    heeled longitudinal sections.39
    integrator method.........41
    metacentric method........37
Steel construction....................61
Table of area curve factors..........75
    data on thirty-footer.......71
    ratios rudder to lateral plane.76
    scantlings for wooden con-
    struction 77
    sizes of keel bolts..........69
    weights of fastenings.......75
    weights of materials........73
    weights of sails............74
    weights of spars...........74
Trapezoidal rule.................... 6
Trochoid, construction of...........22
Versed sines, construction of curve...21
Wave form theory...................21
Wetted surface, area by bilge diago-
    nal method........14
    area by Taylor's
    method 12
Wooden construction..................64